YORK HAND

GENERAL EDITOR:
Professor A.N. Jeffares
(*University of Stirling*)

PREPARING FOR EXAMINATIONS IN ENGLISH LITERATURE

Neil McEwan
MA B LITT (OXFORD)
Lecturer in English, University of Qatar

LONGMAN
YORK PRESS

YORK PRESS
Immeuble Esseily, Place Riad Solh, Beirut

LONGMAN GROUP UK LIMITED
*Longman House, Burnt Mill, Harlow,
Essex CM20 2JE, England
Associated companies, branches and representatives
throughout the world*

© Librairie du Liban 1984

All rights reserved; no part of this publication may be reproduced,
stored in a retrieval system, or transmitted in any form or by any
means, electronic, mechanical, photocopying, recording, or otherwise,
without either the prior written permission of the Publishers or a
licence permitting restricted copying in the United Kingdom issued by
the Copyright Licensing Agency Ltd, 90 Tottenham Court Road, London W1P 9HE.

First published 1984
Fifth impression 1992

ISBN 0-582-03573-2

Printed in Hong Kong
NMW/03

Contents

Part 1: Introduction — *page* 5
  How to use this handbook — 5
  A note on the texts — 10

Part 2: Background to study — 11
  Classical background — 11
    Glossary of Greek and Roman myth and legend — 11
    Ancient literature — 29
  Introduction to English literary history — 34
    The English language in the Middle Ages — 34
    The medieval Church — 35
    Courtly and popular literature — 38
    From the Renaissance to the Restoration — 40
    From the Restoration to the Romantics — 45
    Romanticism — 51
  Glossary of literary terms — 54

Part 3: Working on set-books — 72
  Introduction — 72
  Shakespeare — 74
    Background — 74
    The set-play — 78
  Drama — 80
    Background — 80
    The set-play — 82
  Poetry — 85
  The Novel — 90
    Background — 90
    The set-book — 92
  Revision — 95

Part 4: Written examinations 97
   Context questions and passages for appreciation 97
      Shakespeare 97
      Modern drama 102
      Poetry 105
      Fiction 107
   Essays 111
      Major topic 112
      Minor topic 119
      General topic 124
      Essay topics 131

Part 5: Suggestions for reading 132

Index 137

The author of this Handbook 144

Part 1

Introduction

How to use this handbook

'Only connect' was the motto of the novelist and critic E. M. Forster (1879–1970).* It makes a good rule for study, and for the use of this Handbook. The book's purpose is to help you to plan your work for examinations in English literature, to study with method and purpose, to read with adequate background knowledge, and to avoid wasting time and effort.

Part 2 deals with what you need to know. Any discipline involves the acquisition of basic information and terminology. English studies are now very well supported by reference books and critical commentaries. Even a modest school, college, or university library contains the results of lifetimes of research and compilation. The beginner may easily feel lost. What are you to learn first and how are you to build on that knowledge? More immediately, what is relevant to the texts and authors set for your examination? In answer to these questions, Part 2 provides selected notes and glossaries on classical mythology and literature, on the history of English literature, and on literary terms. Part 3 shows how to apply this background material in approaching set-books. Part 4 shows how to use what you know in writing examinations.

English literature is closely connected with other cultures. If you are studying French or German or Italian you have an advantage which should be developed, for to know any other language and literature is a great help in studying English literature. The second language of most English writers has been Latin. Through Latin even those who, like Shakespeare, have had only a little Greek have become familiar with the poetry, myths and philosophy of ancient Greece. Shakespeare set several of his plays in the ancient world, and in others he drew themes and images from classical sources. One of his earliest plays is based on a Latin comedy (see Part 2, p. 33). Most poets and many playwrights and novelists – including twentieth-century writers – have assumed that the educated reader has some knowledge of Greek and Roman civilisation.

Classical myth and legend has always been a part of English culture. The myths were known in the Middle Ages from Latin sources. In the Renaissance and in the neo-classical period Latin and Greek works were

---

*It is the epigraph to Forster's novel *Howard's End* (1910).

read, translated, and imitated. Although the Romantics rejected many of the precepts of neo-classicism, they did not reject the classics. William Wordsworth's* sonnet 'The World is too much with us' (1807) reflects on the remoteness of nature from the hearts of modern men:

> It [Nature] moves us not. – Great God! I'd rather be
> A pagan suckled in a creed outworn, –
> So might I, standing on this pleasant lea,
> Have glimpses that would make me less forlorn;
> Have sight of Proteus rising from the sea;
> Or hear old Triton blow his wreathèd horn.

Proteus was an old man of the sea, and Triton a sea-god (half dolphin) who blew on a horn of shell. Wordsworth's feeling that pagan antiquity was in close touch with nature was shared by other Romantic and nineteenth-century poets. The Greeks especially were highly thought of in the nineteenth century. In the twentieth century T. S. Eliot and W. B. Yeats have absorbed classical myth into their visions of the modern world. *Ulysses* (1922) by James Joyce is set in twentieth-century Dublin; its characters correspond to figures from Homer's *Odyssey*.

When you refer to the glossary of myths in Part 2, look for connections among the entries. A reference to Atreus will lead you to Menelaus and so to Helen and the whole story of Troy. In this way you will learn or refresh your memory of the myths and so become increasingly independent of glossaries in reading, and perhaps more interested in full-scale studies of myth. The entries in Part 2 cover the names which appear most frequently in English literature.

Notice that myth is treated in various ways. When Shakespeare's King Lear, emerging from madness, tells his daughter: 'thou art a soul in bliss; but I am bound/Upon a wheel of fire, that mine own tears/Do scald like molten lead' (*King Lear* IV.vii.46),† he means that he is in hell. Lear is alluding to Ixion who was punished in the underworld on a burning wheel. Ixion is not referred to but we should recognise the allusion. John Milton refers to classical myths in *Paradise Lost*. The fallen angels who appear in Book I are identified with the gods of Greece and Rome. The first architect who builds in Hell, Milton says, is the angel whom the Romans knew as Mulciber or Vulcan, and the Greeks as Hephaestus:

> Men called him Mulciber; and how he fell
> From Heaven they fabled, thrown by angry Jove
> Sheer o'er the crystal battlements: from morn
> To noon he fell, from noon to dewy eve,
> A summer's day ... Thus they relate,
> Erring   (I.740–7)

*Dates for major writers are provided in Part 2.
†Approximate dates for Shakespeare's plays are given on p. 75.

Although Milton sees the fable as error, his imagination is stirred by the story. Such a reference to myth can be looked up in the glossary in Part 2. Remembering the details will help you to identify allusions. Yeats's sonnet 'Leda and the Swan' (1928) describes the rape of Leda by Zeus in the form of a swan, and alludes to the fact that Leda's daughter by Zeus was Helen:

> A shudder in the loins engenders there
> The broken wall, the burning roof and tower
> And Agamemnon dead.

Looking up Agamemnon would lead you to Troy and so to Helen and her parentage.

The second section of Part 2 is an introduction to English literary history. English literature is more than twelve hundred years old. Although your set-books will probably be chosen from later periods, no writer is independent of the past. The oldest English poetry, from Anglo-Saxon England, has been most influential in the twentieth century. Medieval and Renaissance literature drew on northern European myths of Celtic, Germanic, and Scandinavian origin. Several contemporary writers, including J. R. R. Tolkien (1892–1973), have reworked these legends. Tolkien was Professor of Medieval English Language and Literature at Oxford.

You need to grasp, without being overwhelmed by details, how your set-authors belong to their tradition. William Golding's *Lord of the Flies* (1954) is a contemporary novel, about a group of boys on a tropical island, which can be read without knowledge of previous literature. But when the book is seen in relation to earlier island-stories, to utopian literature from the sixteenth to the twentieth century, and to its philosophical background, it is better understood, and it then makes better reading. (*Lord of the Flies* and its background are discussed in Part 4.) John Milton has a central place in English literature. Studying his poetry involves looking at the conventions of ancient epic, at English allegory, and at the way the Bible has been used in English literature. Students of eighteenth-century verse would want to see how Milton was regarded then. Milton has influenced poets ever since his own time. *Paradise Lost* was reinterpreted in the Romantic period: Satan appealed to the imagination of Romantic writers as a heroic rebel. How to read *Paradise Lost* has been part of the twentieth-century debate about literature. Milton may not be among your set-authors, but he cannot be ignored. No book is independent of the rest of the library. Every period and 'movement' in literature has to be seen in relation to others. Part 2 does not supply a history of English literature, but it shows how to make the necessary connections. Learning names, dates, and the characteristics of periods is no substitute for studying literature, but some facts are a prerequisite to understanding what you read. Further background to Shakespeare and to nineteenth and twentieth-century writers is given in Parts 3 and 4.

The third section of Part 2 is a list of literary terms with brief explanations. Terminology tends to multiply in any subject of study, and to degenerate into jargon. Many excellent critical essays are written in plain English throughout. Specialist vocabulary is often unnecessary. Excessive use of it is unlikely to impress an examiner, but nevertheless some terms must be known. Poetry should not be discussed without taking metre and stanza forms into account. English verse is patterned by stress, and variation of the stress-patterns often means that lines do not exactly fit a metre as it is defined in a text-book. Do not place too much reliance on scansion, but remember that metre does matter. General terms such as 'Romanticism' tend to mean so much that they are impossible to define in a single formula. But they can be most valuable when used with care. English writers have always been relatively independent of schools and movements, but have usually recognised their existence; we need such terms as 'metaphysical' and 'Symbolist', but we should not expect too much of them.

Part 3 is intended to help you to relate this background to your texts. There are three objectives when you approach a set-book:

1. To know the text as thoroughly as possible.
2. To read other books by the same author and of the same period or genre.
3. To read with a view to answering questions effectively.

Close knowledge of the text must come first. Reading other poems, plays, or novels is more worthwhile, and likely to bring better results, than reading criticism. All reading should be done purposefully, and observantly.

Published criticism should come last. When you read a professional critic you enter an extended debate to which the critic's article or book is only a contribution. Taking part requires a wide and detailed knowledge of literature. It is better to read the sources of your Shakespeare play, or another poet of Keats's period, or a second Dickens novel, or to make your own way through the background, than to spend time trying to interpret one stage in a complex argument among scholars.

When you start to read criticism remember that many of the best critics have been creative writers: Samuel Johnson, S. T. Coleridge, T. S. Eliot. Take into account the period at which a critic of the past was writing; eighteenth-century views of Shakespeare are based on different preconceptions from the views of the Romantics. Take one critic at a time and look critically at what is said. Do not underestimate your own judgement – provided you know your author and something of his period. When you differ with a critic, work out why. Part 3 is meant to help you to prepare for reading critics by practising criticism, and by reading intelligently. Francis Bacon's rule that 'some books are to be tasted, others to be swallowed, and some few to be chewed and digested'* is wise. A set-book is to be read carefully more than once; other works by the author and one or more background books should be read through; critics may then be 'tasted'. Part 3 also deals with revision, note-making, and use of libraries.

Part 4 treats the writing of examination answers: there are commentaries on selected passages, and model essays. Examples are taken from books which are frequently set for examinations. The method followed will be clear in each case, even without a previous knowledge of the texts discussed. Part 4 includes advice on planning, selection, use of quotations and background information, comparison, and timing of answers.

Connections need to be made at this stage. While reading Part 4 refer back to earlier Parts. Look up in Part 2 any terms you do not understand. Look up allusions to myth which appear in extracts. Use dictionaries and reference books, following the guidance in Part 3.

When you have studied Part 4, set yourself questions. Consult examination papers from past years and analyse the categories of question: some deal with character or theme; others with period or genre; some ask for contrast or comparison; others for discussion, explanation or illustration. Look again at Part 3. Revise your own notes. Devise systems for connecting various sections of your notes; there can be a mechanical pleasure in this which helps you to learn them. Constantly prune your notes, cutting out what you know and what you are unlikely to need.

Part 5 offers suggestions for reading, based on the fact that wide reading always improves performance in examinations where there is a limited number of set-texts. Answering on Jane Austen's *Pride and Prejudice* (1813) you must write on the book and directly on the question. But you will answer better if you know her *Emma* (1816) and *Persuasion* (1818), and Charlotte Brontë's *Jane Eyre* (1847). It is not a matter of 'dropping' names – examiners can detect that – but you will see the kind of novel *Pride and Prejudice* is when you think of *Jane Eyre* which is very different, and see it more exactly when you think of *Persuasion*, which is less markedly different. Referring to these books in the course of explaining *Pride and Prejudice* is justified and should earn good marks.

Editions are recommended in Part 5 for books discussed in this Handbook. Other works by major authors are proposed as first encounters. A student beginning D. H. Lawrence should read *Sons and*

*Francis Bacon, 'Of Studies', *Essays*, 1597.

Lovers (1913), not *Kangaroo* (1923). *Sons and Lovers* is easier, more characteristic, and a better novel. Paperback collections and series are recommended with a view to your building up a library inexpensively. It is better to own works of literature rather than background books and works of criticism, which you can consult in libraries. If you live near second-hand bookshops you may find cheaper and more durable editions there.

In Part 5, essential reference books are singled out. Every student must own and use at least one good dictionary. A small collection of other literary and linguistic works of reference should be acquired as soon as possible.

This Handbook offers little advice on 'training' for examinations: on keeping fit, relaxing the night before, or sleeping well. But two points are worth making here. The drawback to intense last-minute revision is that you may remember what has been learned in the last twenty-four hours and forget what has been read in the course of the year. A danger in sustained cramming as the examination approaches is that you may lose interest in the books, for a time, and start to resent them. Wide reading, alternated with close study of the texts, prevents staleness. The Handbook is written in the belief that studying literature is pleasant and taking examinations can be a minor pleasure. May you find the same!

A note on the texts

Quotations are from the following sources: *Antony and Cleopatra*, edited by M. R. Ridley, The Arden Shakespeare, Methuen, London, 1954; *King Lear*, edited by Kenneth Muir, The Arden Shakespeare, Methuen, London, 1972; *Othello*, edited by M. R. Ridley, The Arden Shakespeare, Methuen, London, 1958; *Hamlet*, edited by John Dover Wilson, The New Shakespeare, Cambridge University Press, Cambridge, 1934, 1954; John Milton, *Poetical Works*, J. M. Dent, London, 1909; *Collected Poems of Wilfred Owen*, edited by C. Day Lewis, Chatto & Windus, London, 1963; W. B. Yeats, *Collected Poems*, Macmillan, London, 1950; T. S. Eliot, *Collected Poems 1909–1962*, Faber, London, 1963; Oscar Wilde, *The Importance of Being Earnest*, Heinemann, London, 1949; William Golding, *Lord of the Flies*, Faber, London, 1954. The text of the chapter from *Pride and Prejudice* follows R. W. Chapman's edition, Oxford University Press, London, 1923. Quotations from Keats are from *The Poetical Works of John Keats*, edited by H. W. Garrod, The Clarendon Press, Oxford, 1958. Lines from *In Memoriam* are from *Tennyson*, edited by Christopher Ricks, Longman, London, 1969. Lines from Wordsworth, Coleridge, and Shelley are from *The Oxford Book of English Verse of the Romantic Period*, chosen by H. S. Milford, The Clarendon Press, Oxford, 1935.

Part 2

Background to study

Classical background

Glossary of Greek and Roman myth and legend

The glossary which follows has been selected on the basis that the stories referred to are those most frequently used by writers in English literature. All names of characters mentioned in the glossary notes also appear as headwords in their own alphabetical positions. Names in italics in the notes ought to be looked up under their individual headwords since further necessary facts will be found there.

The Romans identified their gods with those of the Greeks (Mars with Ares, Venus with Aphrodite) and they used Latin forms of Greek names for mythic characters (Hercules for Heracles). Both Latin and Greek names are used in English literature. In the glossary the Roman name, where applicable, is given in brackets at the beginning of the Greek entry. Cross-references are provided after the Latin entries.

Achates: *Aeneas*'s faithful friend
Acheron: a river in Hades
Achilles: the greatest Greek warrior at Troy, and a celebrated runner. His mother Thetis dipped him as a child in the river Styx, making him invulnerable except at the heel where she held him; later, when she hid him disguised as a girl to prevent his going to Troy, he was detected by Odysseus. At Troy his slave-girl Briseis was taken by the commander Agamemnon, and he sulked in his tent until enraged when Hector killed his friend Patroclus; then, assisted by his Myrmidons, he slew Hector and dragged the body behind his chariot. He died when Paris wounded him in the heel. His ghost, raised by Odysseus, declared (in Homer's *Odyssey*) that it is better to be the slave of a poor farmer than lord of all the dead. The armour of Achilles was made by Hephaestus. His horses, Xanthus and Balius, were the sons of Zephyrus, the West Wind

12 · Background to study

Acis: a shepherd in Sicily who loved the sea-nymph Galatea. The jealous Cyclops Polyphemus crushed him with a rock, and the nymph turned him into a river

Actaeon: a hunter who spied upon Artemis bathing; as a punishment he was turned into a stag and devoured by his hounds

Adonis: a youth in Cyprus, loved by Aphrodite. He was killed by a boar, and the first anemone grew from his blood. After death he spent six months of each year with Aphrodite, and six months with Persephone in Hades. Flowers and gardens were linked with his worship

Adrastus: see *Epigoni*

Aegisthus: son of Thyestes; see *Agamemnon* and *Orestes*

Aeneas: a Trojan prince; protected by his mother Aphrodite, he escaped after the fall of Troy with his son Ascanius and his father Anchises. His wife Creusa (a daughter of Priam) followed behind and was lost. Aeneas set out with his companions to found a new city. In Carthage Queen Dido fell in love with him; when he left her she killed herself. On a visit to the underworld Aeneas learned that his descendants would rule the future city and empire of Rome. He fought against Turnus, an Italian king, and became king of the Latins. He was known for his piety. (His story is told in Virgil's *Aeneid*)

Aesculapius: the god of medicine, son of Apollo and pupil of Cheiron. Zeus killed him with lightning for restoring Hippolytus to life. Serpents were sacred to him

Agamemnon: a king of Argos; son of Atreus; Menelaus's elder brother. He commanded the Greeks at Troy. He was willing to sacrifice his daughter Iphigenia at Aulis, where the Greek fleet was becalmed, to appease Artemis. On his return after the war he was killed by his wife Clytemnestra and her lover Aegisthus

Ajax: one of the bravest Greeks at Troy. When the arms of the dead Achilles were given to Odysseus he became enraged and killed himself

Alpheus: a river-god who loved the nymph *Arethusa*

Amazons: a race of warrior women, said to have cut off their right breasts to use the bow more effectively. See *Hippolyta* and *Penthesilea*

Anchises:	the father of *Aeneas*
Andromache:	the wife of Hector; she was given to Neoptolemus after the fall of Troy
Andromeda:	she was tied to a rock as a sacrifice to a sea-monster, but was rescued by Perseus
Antigone:	she led her father *Oedipus*, when he was blind, to Colonus. She buried her brother's body, against a king's orders, and killed herself before she could be executed
Aphrodite:	(Venus) the goddess of love and beauty; she was born from the foam of the sea near the island of Cythera. See *Adonis, Ares, Eros, Hephaestus,* and *Paris*
Apollo:	Phoebus Apollo was god of the sun, of plagues, of music and poetry, and of the founding of states. His oracle was at Delphi. Banished by Zeus after a quarrel, he spent nine years as a shepherd. He was the father of Aesculapius. See *Hyacinthus*
Arachne:	she challenged Athene to a weaving contest and was afterwards turned into a spider
Arcadia:	the name of this mountainous region of Greece came to mean an ideal countryside
Ares:	(Mars) the god of war; he was the lover of Aphrodite whose husband Hephaestus caught them in a net, arousing the laughter of the gods
Arethusa:	a nymph, loved by Alpheus, who fled from him to Sicily where Artemis turned her into a stream. Alpheus followed her in the form of a river until they were united
Argonauts:	the companions of *Jason* on the ship Argo; they sought the Golden Fleece at Colchis
Argos:	a monster slain by Hermes; Hera set his hundred eyes in the tail of the peacock
Ariadne:	the daughter of Minos; she loved *Theseus*, assisted him in the labyrinth at Crete, and killed herself when he abandoned her
Arion:	a poet who was carried ashore by a dolphin (which had been charmed by his singing) after sailors had thrown him overboard
Artemis:	(Diana) twin sister of Apollo; a virgin huntress, later identified with the moon. She assisted distressed virgins. See *Actaeon, Arethusa, Agamemnon, Iphigenia, Leto, Niobe*
Ascanius:	the son of *Aeneas*

Atalanta: a swift runner, she was reluctant to marry. She obliged her suitors to race with her; when they lost she killed them. She was outwitted and outrun by Milanion who distracted her by throwing down golden apples. She hunted the boar of Calydon with *Meleager*
Ate: the goddess of evil
Athene: (Minerva) the goddess of wisdom: sometimes called Pallas. She gave her name to Athens and was its protector
Atlas: a *Titan* punished by having to hold up the heavens. He was turned into a mountain by *Perseus*
Atreus: a king of Argos. When his brother Thyestes seduced his wife he offered him his own children cooked at a banquet. Thyestes put a curse on his descendants. Atreus was killed by Thyestes's son Aegisthus. See *Agamemnon* and *Menelaus*
Atropos: see *Fates*
Augean stables: see *Heracles*
Aurora: see *Eos*
Autolycus: a thief, expert in stealing sheep. When he stole those of Sisyphus king of Corinth he was found out because Sisyphus had marked their feet
Bacchus: see *Dionysus*
Balius: one of the horses of Achilles. See *Xanthus* and *Zephyrus*
Basilisk: (or Cockatrice) a monster whose gaze was fatal
Baucis: see *Philemon* and *Baucis*
Bellerophon: as a guest at the court of Proetus at Tiryns he rejected the queen's advances. She complained to her husband that he had tried to seduce her. Proetus sent him to his father-in-law Iobates with a letter asking for Bellerophon's death. Iobates required him to fight the *Chimaera*, which he destroyed with the help of the winged horse Pegasus. After other adventures he married Iobates's daughter
Briseis: see *Achilles*
Cadmus: a Phoenician who founded Thebes with men who grew from the dragon's teeth he planted there. He brought the alphabet to Greece
Calliope: see *Muses*
Callisto: a nymph loved by Zeus. Hera turned her into a bear. She became the constellation called the Great Bear
Calydon: see *Atalanta* and *Meleager*

Background to study · 15

Calypso: a nymph, a daughter of Atlas; she offered Odysseus immortality if he would stay with her
Cassandra: a daughter of Priam. Her prophecies of the fall of Troy were not believed
Castor and Pollux: twins, sons of Zeus and Leda. They accompanied the Argonauts, and became the constellation of the Twins (Gemini)
Centaurs: they were men to the waist and horses below. See *Cheiron* and *Nessus*
Cerberus: the many-headed guard-dog of Hades. See *Heracles*
Ceres: see *Demeter*
Charon: the ferryman on the Styx in Hades. He had to be paid with a coin (an 'obol') which the dead took with them
Charybdis: a woman turned into a whirlpool. See *Scylla*
Cheiron: a learned *centaur*. He taught Aesculapius medicine and was tutor to Achilles and Jason. Heracles accidentally caused his death
Chimaera: a monster. Its body was a goat's; its tail a dragon's; its head (which spouted flames) a lion's. *Bellerophon* killed it
Cimmerians: a people who lived in permanent darkness
Circe: a witch who turned the companions of Odysseus into swine. Odysseus preserved himself with a herb ('Moly'), then compelled Circe to restore his men
Clio: see *Muses*
Clotho: see *Fates*
Clytemnestra: the wife and (with her lover Aegisthus) murderer of *Agamemnon*. See *Orestes*
Cockatrice: see *Basilisk*
Cocles, Horatius: he held the Tiber bridge at Rome against Lars Porsena until it fell and he swam ashore in his armour
Cocytus: a river in Hades
Colchis: see *Jason*
Colonus: Oedipus, blind, came here to die
Corybantes: priests of Cybele, noted for their extravagant and orgiastic rituals. Often confused with *Curetes*
Creusa: the wife of *Aeneas*
Cronos: (Saturn) a *Titan*. The father of Zeus whom he intended to eat as a baby. Zeus overthrew and succeeded him as king of the gods
Cumae: see *Sibyls*
Cupid: see *Eros*

16 · Background to study

Curetes:	young men summoned to protect the infant Zeus from *Cronos*; they kept him on Mount Ida and covered his cries with the clashing of their weapons. Often confused with *Corybantes*
Cybele:	Asian 'Mother of Gods', identified by the Greeks with *Rhea*
Cyclops:	one-eyed giants in Sicily. They made the thunderbolts of Zeus. See *Polyphemus*
Daedalus:	an Athenian craftsman who built a labyrinth in Crete for King Minos. Later he escaped from Crete on artificial wings. See *Icarus*
Danae:	confined by her father (a king of Argos) in a bronze tower, she was raped by Zeus in the form of a shower of gold, becoming the mother of Perseus
Daphne:	fleeing from Apollo she was turned into a laurel
Daphnis:	a Sicilian shepherd, taught the flute by Pan; he invented pastoral poetry
Deianira:	see *Heracles* and *Nessus*
Delphi:	the site of an oracle sacred to *Apollo*
Demeter:	(Ceres) the goddess of agriculture, and mother of Persephone
Deucalion:	he and his wife Pyrrha survived a flood which covered the earth. Afterwards they threw stones which became people and restored the human race
Diana:	see *Artemis*
Dido:	a queen of Carthage. See *Aeneas*
Dionysus:	also called Bacchus; the god of wine and revelry, fertility, ecstasy, and rebirth. His chariot was drawn by wild animals
Dis:	see *Pluto*
Dryads and Hamadryads:	tree-nymphs
Electra:	a daughter of Agamemnon. She encouraged Orestes to avenge their father's murder by killing *Clytemnestra*. She married Orestes's comrade Pylades
Endymion:	a shepherd with whom *Selene* (or Artemis) fell in love and put to sleep for ever so that she might admire him
Eos:	(Aurora) the goddess of dawn. See *Tithonus*
Epigoni:	the descendants of the *Seven Against Thebes*, who, led by Adrastus, marched against Thebes and destroyed it
Epimetheus:	the brother of Prometheus and husband of *Pandora*
Erato:	see *Muses*

Eros:	(Cupid) son of Aphrodite; the god of love: a blind, winged boy with bow and arrows. See *Psyche*
Eteocles:	see *Seven Against Thebes*
Eumenides:	Furies, known (by this name) as the 'Kindly Ones' – from fear of causing offence. They pursued criminals and caused plagues and disasters
Euridice:	the wife of Orpheus. After death she was to have been released from Hades, on condition that as she followed behind him he did not look back. He failed, and she remained
Europa:	a king's daughter loved by Zeus who approached her in the form of a bull. He carried her to Crete. She became the mother of Minos and Rhadamanthus
Euterpe:	see *Muses*
Fates:	Clotho, Lachesis and Atropos, represented as three old women spinning cloth. Their role was to allot the fate of every individual
Fauns:	Roman *satyrs*
Faunus:	a Roman nature god
Furies:	see *Eumenides*
Galatea:	(i) a nymph loved by *Acis*; (ii) a statue which came to life, made by *Pygmalion*
Ganymede(s):	a shepherd-boy loved by Zeus whose eagle lifted him from Mount Ida to Olympus. He succeeded Hebe as cupbearer to the gods
Ge:	an earth goddess; see *Uranus* and *Titans*
Giants:	they fought against Zeus and the gods and were confined in the earth after their defeat. See *Pelion*
Glaucus:	(i) a sea god; (ii) the father of Bellerophon; (iii) a warrior who fought with the Trojans
Golden Fleece:	the fleece of a flying ram which had been sacrificed to Zeus. See *Argonauts* and *Jason*
Gorgons:	three monstrous sisters. Serpents grew from their heads; their gaze turned the living to stone. See *Medusa*
Gyges:	a shepherd who murdered the king of Lydia and married the queen, aided by a brazen ring which made him invisible. In another version he was a friend of the king, who allowed him to see the queen naked; afterwards she persuaded him to kill her husband
Hades:	the underworld. See *Pluto*
Hebe:	the goddess of youth, and (before Ganymedes) cupbearer to the gods

Hecate:	the triple-formed goddess of night and witchcraft
Hector:	a son of Priam; the husband of Andromache. He was a great Trojan warrior, slain by Achilles
Hecuba:	the wife of *Priam*
Helen:	the loveliest of women, daughter of Zeus and Leda. After marriage to *Menelaus* she was taken to Troy by *Paris* and so was the cause of the Trojan War. Afterwards she returned to Menelaus
Hephaestus:	(Vulcan or Mulciber) the god of fire and metalwork. A son of Hera, he was thrown from Olympus by Zeus when he took his mother's side in a quarrel. He fell for nine days, and was lamed when he dropped on Lesbos. His wife Aphrodite was unfaithful to him with Ares: he caught them together, in a net. Hephaestus made the armour of Achilles
Hera:	(Juno) the sister and jealous wife of Zeus. See *Hephaestus* and *Paris*
Heracles:	(Hercules) a son of Zeus, and a hero. As an infant he crushed snakes in his hands. He chose Virtue rather than Pleasure as a course of life. He performed twelve labours. The best known are: cleansing the stables of Augeas (by diverting a river through them); winning golden apples from the Garden of the Hesperides; bringing Cerberus up from Hades; killing the *Hydra* (with whose poisonous blood he tipped his arrows). He parted the straits of Gibraltar, and performed many other wonders. He died in the poisoned cloak of *Nessus*, sent by his wife Deianira. See *Lichas*, *Hylas* and *Prometheus*
Hercules:	see *Heracles*
Hermaphroditus:	his body was merged with that of a nymph who loved him
Hermes:	(Mercury) the messenger of the gods. He was also god of luck, of wealth, of travels, of merchants, and of thieves; he led the dead to Hades. He is pictured wearing winged sandals
Hermione:	the daughter of Menelaus and Helen. She married Neoptolemus and, later, Orestes
Hero:	a priestess of Aphrodite at Sestos on the Hellespont straits. She used to guide her lover Leander with a torch as he swam the straits to join her. One night he drowned and she threw herself into the sea
Hesperides:	the golden apples of the Garden of the Hesperides were guarded by a dragon. See *Heracles*

Hesperus:	the evening star, which is Venus
Hestia:	goddess of the hearth
Hippolyta:	queen of the Amazons and wife of *Theseus*
Hippolytus:	a son of Theseus and Hippolyta. He rejected the advances of his stepmother Phaedra who turned Theseus against him. He was killed when his chariot encountered a sea-monster sent by Poseidon in response to Theseus's prayer for vengeance
Hyacinthus:	a boy loved by Apollo and Zephyrus. When he preferred Apollo, Zephyrus turned the flight of a discus so that it killed Hyacinthus. Apollo made the hyacinth from his blood
Hydra:	a many-headed monster; when one head was cut off, two grew in its place. The Hydra was destroyed by *Heracles*
Hylas:	a boy loved by Heracles; he was lured by nymphs into a fountain and drowned. In his grief Heracles abandoned the Argonauts
Hyperion:	a *Titan*, father of sun and moon; the sun-god who was succeeded by Apollo
Icarus:	a boy, the son of *Daedalus*. When they escaped from Crete on wings fastened with wax, he flew too near the sun; the wax melted and he fell into the sea
Ichor:	the immortal blood of the gods
Ida:	a mountain near Troy from which the gods watched the war. See *Ganymedes*, *Oenone*, and *Paris*
Iobates:	see *Bellerophon*
Iolchis:	see *Jason*
Iphigenia:	she vanished when her father *Agamemnon* had agreed to her sacrifice at Aulis and a deer took her place. Artemis placed her at Tauris where she was obliged to sacrifice all strangers. When her brother *Orestes* came, seeking to purify himself, she escaped with him, taking away the statue of Artemis which the oracle of Delphi had instructed Orestes to bring to Greece
Ithaca:	the island ruled by *Odysseus*
Itys:	see *Philomela*
Ixion:	treacherous in life, he was bound to a wheel of fire in Hades
Janus:	the Roman god of gates, and of the year (hence January). In wartime his temple-gates were open; they were closed in peace. He had two faces (in statues) looking opposite ways

Jason:	the leader of the Argonauts. When he demanded the Kingdom of Iolchis, usurped by his uncle, he was challenged to recapture a golden fleece at Colchis – for the sake of which a kinsman had been killed. He sailed in the ship Argo and, helped by the sorceress *Medea*, performed heroic deeds and won the golden fleece
Jocasta:	see *Oedipus*
Jove:	see *Zeus*
Juno:	see *Hera*
Jupiter:	see *Zeus*
Kraken:	a sea-monster
Lachesis:	see *Fates*
Laertes:	the father of *Odysseus*
Laius:	see *Oedipus*
Laocoön:	a Trojan priest of Apollo who was killed (with his two sons) by a sea-serpent after trying to dissuade the Trojans from accepting the Wooden Horse. See *Troy*
Latona:	see *Leto*
Leander:	see *Hero*
Leda:	ravished by Zeus (in the form of a swan), she was the mother of Helen and of Castor and Pollux
Lethe:	a river in Hades; its waters gave the power to forget
Leto:	(Latona) Mother of Apollo and Artemis. See *Tityrus*
Lichas:	he brought the poisoned cloak of *Nessus* to his master *Heracles*, who threw him into the sea
Lotus-eaters:	a people encountered by Odysseus. When his men ate the lotus they lost all wish to return home
Lucifer:	see *Phosphorus*
Lucrece:	a virtuous Roman lady who killed herself after being raped by Sextus, son of *Tarquin*
Luna:	see *Selene*
Maenads:	priestesses of *Dionysus*
Manes:	spirits of the dead revered by the Romans
Mars:	see *Ares*
Marsyas:	he challenged Apollo to a trial of skill in pipe-playing. Apollo won and then flayed him alive for his effrontery
Medea:	a ruthless princess and magician of Colchis, she was the lover of *Jason*. When he abandoned her for a princess of Corinth she killed their children in revenge

Medusa:	a *Gorgon* slain by *Perseus* who used the head as a weapon: it turned all living things to stone
Meleager:	a hero and Argonaut who slew a dangerous boar in the region of Calydon and presented its head to Atalanta. A quarrel followed in which he killed his uncles. His mother then destroyed a burning brand, believed to preserve him, and he died when the brand was gone
Melpomene:	see *Muses*
Menelaus:	a king of Sparta; a son of *Atreus*, the brother of *Agamemnon* and the husband of *Helen*. He was among the best Greek warriors at Troy
Mentor:	a friend of Odysseus. Pretending to be him, Athene accompanied and counselled *Telemachus*
Mercury:	see *Hermes*
Midas:	Dionysus granted his wish that all he touched would turn to gold. Apollo gave him the ears of an ass
Milanion:	see *Atalanta*
Minerva:	see *Athene*
Minos:	King of Crete. In one legend he was so just a ruler that he became judge of the dead in Hades. In another he was the master of the *Minotaur* for which he provided seven youths and seven girls from Athens every year. See *Theseus*
Minotaur:	a bull-like monster, son by Minos's wife Pasiphae of a white bull sacred to Poseidon. It occupied a labyrinth constructed by Daedalus. The Minotaur was destroyed by *Theseus*
Mnemosyne:	her name means 'memory'; she was, by Zeus, the mother of the *Muses*
Moly:	see *Circe*
Mulciber:	see *Hephaestus*
Muses:	the nine Muses who inspired artists and poets were born in Pieria near Olympus. Clio was the Muse of history; the others were: Euterpe (lyric poetry); Thalia (comedy and pastoral); Melpomene (tragedy); Terpsichore (dancing); Erato (love-poetry); Polyhymnia (sacred song); Urania (astronomy); and Calliope (epic poetry)
Myrmidons:	followers of *Achilles* at Troy
Naiads:	river-nymphs
Narcissus:	he fell in love with his reflection in water and was drowned
Nausicaa:	see *Phaeacians*

Neoptolemus:	also called Pyrrhus, the (yellow-haired) son of Achilles. He slew Priam, took possession of Andromache, married Hermione, and was killed by Orestes
Neptune:	see *Poseidon*
Nereids:	sea-nymphs
Nessus:	a *centaur* who carried Deianira across a river, then assaulted her and was shot by her husband Heracles. Dying, he gave Deianira his cloak – poisoned by the arrow – telling her it would restore an unfaithful husband. Later, she sent it to Heracles. See *Lichas*
Nestor:	the oldest and wisest of the Greeks at Troy
Niobe:	her twelve children were killed by Artemis and Apollo when she claimed to be greater than their mother Leto. She was turned to stone but continued to weep for her children
Numa:	the second King of Rome and founder of the Roman religion
Oceanus:	a *Titan* and father of the gods
Odysseus:	(Ulysses) a king of Ithaca; the wiliest of the Greeks. His adventures on the long journey home from Troy are narrated in Homer's *Odyssey*. See *Calypso*, *Circe*, *Penelope*, *Phaeacians*, *Polyphemus*, and *Telemachus*
Oedipus:	he fulfilled a prophecy when he unknowingly killed his father Laius, King of Thebes, and married his mother Jocasta. When he learned the truth he blinded himself. See *Antigone* and *Sphinx*
Oenone:	a nymph of Mount Ida with powers of prophecy and medicine, loved and abandoned by *Paris*
Olympic Games:	thought to have been founded by Heracles, they were held every four years and provided the Greeks with their system of dating
Olympus:	this north-eastern mountain was the home of the gods
Oreads:	nymphs of the mountains
Orestes:	he avenged the murder of his father *Agamemnon* by killing his mother *Clytemnestra* and her lover Aegisthus. He was helped in his adventures by Pylades, a close friend with whom he had grown up. See *Iphigenia*, *Electra*, *Hermione* and *Neoptolemus*
Orpheus:	the son of the *Muse* Calliope, he was a poet and musician whose performance on the lyre entranced

	even wild animals. He helped the Argonauts to resist the Sirens. After his failure to rescue his dead wife *Euridice* from Hades he took to the wilderness where he was torn to pieces by wild women
Ossa:	see *Pelion*
Pallas:	see *Athene*
Pan:	the horned, goat-footed god of shepherds and huntsmen. He invented the reed-flute. He caused panics
Pandora:	the first woman, she was made by Hephaestus when Zeus had been angered by *Prometheus*'s work on behalf of men. She received gifts from the gods, and from Zeus a box, as a dowry. Her husband, Prometheus's brother Epimetheus, opened the box from which all human ills came forth. Hope was found at the bottom of the box
Paris:	a son of *Priam*, brought up by shepherds on Mount Ida (having been put out to die after a prophecy that he would cause Troy's fall). He judged a beauty contest among the goddesses Hera, Athene, and Aphrodite, to whom he awarded the title. His first love was Oenone. Later he seduced *Helen* in Sparta and took her from her husband Menelaus. Oenone refused to help him when he was fatally wounded by the bow of Philoctetes
Parnassus:	a sacred mountain, north of Delphi; the home of the *Muses*
Pasiphae:	see *Minotaur*
Patroclus:	a Greek warrior at Troy and the close friend of *Achilles*. When he was killed by Hector, Achilles returned to the fighting to avenge him
Pegasus:	a winged horse, born from the blood of *Medusa*. See *Bellerophon* and *Chimaera*
Peirithous:	see *Theseus*
Pelion:	the giants, fighting the gods, heaped Mount Ossa upon Mount Pelion to reach Heaven
Pelops:	Pelops was killed by his father, *Tantalus*, who served him to the gods at a banquet. They restored him to life, and remade his shoulder – consumed by Demeter – with ivory. His house was cursed after his treachery over a chariot race. His sons were Atreus and Thyestes
Penelope:	the wife of *Odysseus*. During his absence she was beset by suitors. She told them she would make her

Penthesilea:
choice when she had finished work on a tapestry; at night she undid what she had woven during the day. When Odysseus returned he slew the suitors. See *Telemachus*
a queen of the *Amazons* who fought for Troy after Hector's death and was killed by Achilles. See *Thersites*

Persephone:
(Proserpine) a daughter of Zeus and Demeter. Pluto carried her off from the Sicilian region of Enna, to Hades. Demeter eventually persuaded Zeus to grant Persephone six months of each year in this world; she passed the remaining (winter) months in the underworld

Perseus:
the son of Zeus and *Danae*. The gods assisted him in a quest for the head of Medusa. When badly received by Atlas, Perseus used the severed head to turn him to stone. He also petrified the sea-monster which threatened *Andromeda*

Phaeacians:
a seafaring people of the West visited by the shipwrecked Odysseus; he was found on the shore by the king's daughter Nausicaa

Phaedra:
a daughter of Minos and Pasiphae, she was the wife of Theseus. See *Hyppolytus*

Phaeton:
a boy who persuaded his father, Apollo, to let him drive the sun-chariot; he was struck dead by Zeus when his failure to control it endangered the world

Phaon:
an old, ugly boatman who refused payment from Aphrodite disguised as a poor old woman; he was given youth and good looks in return

Philemon and Baucis: a virtuous old couple who received the disguised Zeus and Hermes with hospitality and were rewarded

Philoctetes:
left wounded on an island but later brought to Troy by Odysseus because he owned the bow and arrows of Heracles; with these he shot Paris

Philomela:
her sister Procne was married to Tereus who raped Philomela, cut out her tongue, and imprisoned her. She managed to send Procne a tapestry showing what had happened. Procne served the flesh of her son Itys to Tereus. Before he could retaliate he was turned into a hoopoe; Procne became a swallow; Philomela a nightingale

Phlegethon:
a river of fire in Hades

Phoebus:
see *Apollo*

Phoenix: a fabulous bird which died by fire every five hundred years; a new phoenix rose from the ashes
Phorcis: a sea-god, father of the *Gorgons*
Phosphorus: (Lucifer) the morning star, which is Venus
Pieria: a shrine of the *Muses* near Olympus
Pleiades: the seven daughters of *Atlas*; they became a group of stars after death
Pluto: also known as Hades and as Dis. The brother of Zeus and Poseidon, he was god of the underworld (Hades). See *Persephone* and *Orpheus*
Plutus: a son of Demeter; the blind, lamed, winged god of riches
Pollux: see *Castor and Pollux*
Polyhymnia: see *Muses*
Polyneices: see *Seven Against Thebes*
Polyphemus: a son of Poseidon; a *Cyclops*. He loved the nymph Galatea and killed her lover Acis. He was blinded in his one eye by Odysseus, whose men he was devouring; Odysseus escaped by clinging to one of Polyphemus's rams
Pomona: a Roman goddess of gardens
Porsena, Lars: an Etruscan King who attacked Rome seeking to restore *Tarquin*; he was resisted at the bridge by Horatius *Cocles*
Poseidon: (Neptune) the brother of Zeus and Pluto, and god of the sea. He helped to build the walls of Troy and afterwards opposed the Trojans because he had not been rewarded
Priam: the last king of Troy, killed at the fall of the city. He had over fifty children including *Paris*, *Hector*, and *Cassandra*. After Hector's death Priam visited the tent of Achilles to beg for his body
Priapus: a fertility god
Procne: see *Philomela*
Procrustes: a Greek brigand killed by Theseus. He fitted his prisoners to the length of a bed by cutting short their legs or stretching their bodies
Proetus: see *Bellerophon*
Prometheus: a son of the Titans, he created men from clay and taught them skills. He stole fire from heaven and brought it to earth. This so angered Zeus that he created *Pandora* and chained Prometheus to a rock where his liver was consumed daily by a vulture. He was rescued by Heracles

Proserpine:	see *Persephone*
Proteus:	Poseidon's shepherd; he had prophetic gifts but assumed a 'protean' variety of forms to escape those who tried to question him
Psyche:	she was the lover of Cupid in a late Roman allegorical story. She angered Cupid by spilling oil from a lamp on his sleeping body. After this, Venus tormented her. She was eventually reunited with Cupid
Pygmalion:	a king of Cyprus who fell in love with a sculpture of a girl (his own work). Aphrodite brought it to life as Galatea
Pylades:	the friend of *Orestes*
Pyrrha:	the wife of *Deucalion*
Pyrrhus:	see *Neoptolemus*
Pythia:	Apollo's priestess at Delphi
Python:	a serpent born from slime after Deucalion's flood; it was killed by Apollo
Quirinus:	a Roman god, identified eventually with *Romulus* after the latter's death
Remus:	see *Romulus*
Rhadamanthus:	a judge in Hades
Rhea:	a *Titan*, the wife of Cronos, and mother of Zeus. The Greeks later identified her with the Asian goddess Cybele
Romulus:	a son of Mars, he was the founder of Rome. He and his twin Remus were abandoned in childhood and suckled by a she-wolf. When Romulus had begun to build the Roman walls Remus jumped over them in mockery and Romulus killed him
Sabines:	they went to war against the Romans who had carried off their women. Later they settled in Rome
Sarpedon:	a Lydian prince who fought with the Trojans and was killed by *Patroclus*
Saturn:	see *Cronos*
Satyr:	a creature of the woods, partly human and partly horse (partly goat in Roman art). They were followers of *Dionysus*, and known for their dancing and sensuality
Scylla:	a nymph loved by Poseidon. Bewitched by Circe, she became a monster at the straits of Messina opposite the whirlpool Charybdis
Selene:	(Luna) a moon goddess, later identified with *Artemis*

Background to study · 27

Semele: she was killed by the lightning of Zeus when she prayed that he visit her in the form of a god. Their child was Dionysus, whom Zeus snatched from her womb and preserved in his own thigh until his birth

Seven Against Thebes: an army led by seven heroes marched against Thebes when Eteocles (son of Oedipus and Jocasta) refused to give up the throne for alternate years – as had been agreed – to his brother Polyneices. The brothers killed each other in a tournament. (*Seven Against Thebes* was a play by Aeschylus)

Silenus: a *satyr* attendant on *Dionysus*

Sinon: see *Troy*

Sibyls: wise-women. The sibyl at Cumae in Italy was cursed with a life centuries long without youth or health. She led Aeneas to the underworld, and sold three prophetic books to Tarquin

Sirens: (i) their songs lured sailors to shipwreck; (ii) (in the works of Plato) heavenly singers

Sisyphus: King of Corinth. In Hades he was condemned eternally to roll a stone to a hilltop, from which it always rolled back. He was the father of Sinon

Sphinx: a Theban monster (part-lion, part-woman) which posed riddles and killed those who could not answer. It killed itself when Oedipus solved a riddle

Stentor: a Greek warrior at Troy whose voice was as strong as the voices of fifty men together. He perished when he challenged Hermes to a shouting contest

Styx: a river in Hades over which the dead were ferried by Charon. The gods swore oaths by the Styx

Syrinx: fleeing from Pan she was changed into a reed

Talus: (i) a brass man made by Hephaestus. He protected Crete at the time of Minos by embracing strangers, when red hot. He attacked the Argonauts with rocks; (ii) a craftsman and rival of Daedalus who killed him

Tantalus: he was punished, for his treatment of his son *Pelops* (and for thefts from the gods), by hunger and thirst in Hades where food and water were always just out of his reach

Tarquin: Tarquinius Superbus (son of Tarquinius Priscus, a wise king) was an oppressive king of Rome. His son Sextus raped Lucrece and the Tarquins were driven from Rome. He bought three prophetic books from the Sibyl of Cumae

Tartarus:	the region of Hades where the guilty were punished
Telemachus:	when his father Odysseus failed to come home after the fall of Troy, Telemachus (guided by Athene in the form of Mentor) went to search for him, in vain. He returned to Ithaca in time to join Odysseus in killing the suitors who had beset his mother Penelope
Tempe:	a beautiful valley between Olympus and Ossa
Tereus:	see *Philomela*
Terpsichore:	see *Muses*
Tethys:	a sea goddess
Teucer:	the best archer among the Greeks at Troy
Thalia:	see *Muses*
Thamyris:	a poet who challenged the Muses and was blinded
Thebes:	a city in Boeotia in Greece. See *Cadmus* and *Oedipus*
Thersites:	a foul-mouthed Greek at Troy, killed by Achilles for scoffing at his grief for Penthesilea
Theseus:	an heroic king of Athens who destroyed many monsters and criminals. He killed the *Minotaur* in Crete helped by Ariadne who gave him a thread with which to escape from the labyrinth. He carried off and married Hippolyta. He went to the underworld with Peirithous to release Persephone and was confined there until rescued by Heracles. See *Hippolytus*
Thetis:	a sea goddess and mother of *Achilles*
Thyestes:	see *Atreus*
Tiresias:	a prophet who gave counsel in Thebes. In one story he was blinded because he saw Athene bathing. In another he was, for a time, a woman. He lived for many generations and continued to give prophecies in Hades
Titans:	the children of *Uranus* and Ge, who included Cronos, Rhea, Oceanus and Hyperion. When they overthrew Uranus, Cronos became king of the gods. Zeus in turn overthrew his father Cronos and a new order of gods succeeded the Titans
Tithonus:	Tithonus was given immortality by Eos (Aurora), who loved him, but he failed to ask for immortal youth
Tityrus:	a giant who attacked Leto and was killed by Apollo and Artemis. In Hades his liver was perpetually gnawed by vultures
Triton:	a sea god, half-dolphin

Troy:	an ancient city in north-west Asia Minor. According to Homer it was besieged for ten years by a Greek army, after the elopement of *Helen* with *Paris*. The city was taken when the Greeks withdrew leaving a large wooden horse full of armed men which Sinon, a Greek who had pretended to join the Trojans, persuaded them to pull within the walls. At night Sinon opened the horse. See *Achilles*, *Agamemnon*, *Hector*, *Menelaus*, *Priam*, *Odysseus*
Turnus:	an Italian king who fought against *Aeneas*
Ulysses:	see *Odysseus*
Urania:	see *Muses*
Uranus:	god of the sky and oldest of the gods; the husband of Ge (the earth) and father of the *Titans*
Venus:	see *Aphrodite*
Vertumnus:	the Roman god of seasons and fruits; he loved and pursued *Pomona*
Vesta:	the Roman goddess of hearth and home. Her temple flame was kept by the Vestal Virgins (upper-class Roman women pledged to religious celibacy)
Vulcan:	see *Hephaestus*
Xanthus:	one of Achilles's talking horses; the other was Balius
Zephyrus:	the West Wind; he was the father of the horses of Achilles. See *Hyacinthus*
Zeus:	the son of *Cronos* and Rhea and king of the gods after his overthrow of Cronos. He gave the seas to his brother Poseidon and the underworld to his brother Pluto. He married his sister Hera. He loved mortal girls, and took various shapes to win them: Leda, as a swan; Danae as a shower of gold; Europa, as a bull. In one version of the story he took the form of an eagle to carry off Ganymedes. Zeus was the god of thunder. He was omnipotent – except that he could not control Fate, who was said to stand behind his throne

Ancient literature

The legends referred to in the glossary above have been a source of inspiration throughout the history of literature. They once encoded the rituals and lore of primitive peoples. Their human interest and artistic possibilities were understood by the earliest European authors. Later writers, even when (for various reasons) they have disapproved of 'paganism', have followed the example of Greek and Roman poets and dramatists.

Homer made more of myth than any of those who came after him. We know nothing about his life. According to tradition he was blind and destitute, although seven cities claimed him after his death. Some scholars have doubted his existence, arguing that the *Iliad* and *Odyssey* belong to an oral tradition in which stories and style were held in common among singers, and were not the work of an individual. Today it is thought that Homer lived in the ninth century BC, and that he brought his own art and knowledge of life to these written versions of older oral cycles of narrative poetry. Homer's world is remote: his heroes Achilles and Odysseus belong to an aristocratic warrior-caste which lives by war; they strive for glory while the gods look on and sometimes intervene. But the poems have always been found compelling by readers in societies quite unlike Homer's. His work has influenced English epic and mock-epic, romance, drama, and the distinctly modern genre of the novel.

A modern reader who objects to the childishness of the myths should remember that such scepticism began among the Greeks. The poet Xenophanes (576–480BC) objected: 'Homer ascribed to the gods things that are a disgrace among mortals: thefts and adulteries and deceptions.' In the centuries after Homer many intellectuals looked for explanations of the world in science rather than in myth. Even a generation before Xenophanes, the philosopher Thales (born about 624BC) was doing so; he predicted, by observation, an eclipse of the sun. But the mythic view of life was not abandoned; it was explored, several centuries after Homer, by the tragic dramatists of Athens.

Aeschylus (525–456BC) is the earliest tragedian. Seven of his plays survive, including a trilogy (*Agamemnon, The Libation-Bearers, The Eumenides*) on the story of how Orestes avenged his father Agamemnon. It shows the triumphant return of Agamemnon from Troy, and his murder by his wife Clytemnestra and her lover Aegisthus. Orestes's act of vengeance in killing his mother and his pursuit by the Furies are followed by a trial in which Athene presides over the outcome. Questions of justice arise, of the nature of family ties, and of duty in conflict with emotion. Aeschylus takes the legends seriously. The 'Oresteian Trilogy' is the best introduction to Greek tragedy.

Those who go no further will have seen how in Greek tragedy poetry is combined with dialogue, violent action with bold ideas, interest in men and women with speculation about the gods. Those who wish to go on should read Sophocles's *Oedipus, Oedipus at Colonus* and *Antigone*. Sophocles (496–406BC) increased the number of actors (apart from the chorus) and developed the study of character in drama. But many readers consider *The Bacchae* by Euripides (480–406BC) the greatest Greek tragedy. Pentheus, King of Thebes, rejects the worship of Dionysus; the god drives him mad; Dionysus's followers (the Bacchanals) tear him to pieces. Euripides's *The Trojan Women* shows the fates of women of the royal family just after the fall of Troy. The play is impressive for its psychology (especially in the characters of Hecuba and Helen), for its sympathy with women, and for its evocation of the horror and pity of war. Euripides is realistic about men and women; and, perhaps, sceptical about the gods.

The comic dramatist Aristophanes ($c.448-c.380$BC) satirised contemporary events and individuals (including Euripides). But even without much background knowledge readers can find him exhilarating. In *The Birds* two Athenians, weary of the social and political troubles of their city, visit Tereus (the king who was changed into a hoopoe after raping Philomela), seeking rest among the birds. They soon persuade the birds to form their own city-state and an empire of the skies, in defiance of men and gods. Aristophanes shows how quickly the desire for peace is forgotten in the will to power. Political satire is blended with lyricism: the chorus of birds contemplate the unhappy earthbound condition of men. Social realism and sexual frankness are blended with poetry and fantasy. In Aristophanes's *The Frogs* Dionysus visits Hades, where a chorus of frogs greets him as he travels in Charon's boat. A drama contest takes place between Aeschylus and Euripides, who are now among the dead: each ridicules the other's work. Aeschylus's work is slow and arrogantly aristocratic, Euripides claims; Euripides has debased tragedy and corrupted the Athenians, says Aeschylus. Good writing, Aristophanes asserts, and good judgement must return to the city imperilled by a long, losing war with Sparta. Like *The Birds*, *The Frogs* can easily be read for pleasure. Both plays impress modern readers with the power all Greek writers possessed to see as a whole what to us are separate aspects of life. For the Greeks, literary and political values are closely connected. Coarse jokes and poetry can go together. Harmony is the chief virtue.

Plato and Aristotle are names which English students will meet frequently. The dialogues of the philosopher Plato ($c.427-348$BC), based on the ideas of Socrates (469–399BC), are the origin of much of European thought. Beginners might read the *Apology* in which Socrates defends himself at the trial where he is condemned to death for impiety. Plato taught that our world is one of appearances behind which lie the real *ideas* or *forms* of things. Good is the supreme idea and to know that is to seek the good. Virtue and true knowledge are the same. Another of Plato's most influential (and controversial) concepts is that of the state as a tightly organised body fully responsible for its members. He held that poets would have to be excluded from an ideal Republic.

Aristotle (384–322BC), who declared that he loved Plato but loved truth more, was a logician, a natural scientist, a moral philosopher, a political scientist, and a literary critic. Among English students, the views on tragedy in his *Poetics* are still widely discussed. He defined a tragedy as an imitation of an action which is serious and self-contained, taking the form of drama (not narrative), and arousing fear and pity to achieve *catharsis*: the purging of these emotions. He argued for logic in development of the plot and for a single action. The tragic hero, he said, must pass from happiness to misery as a result of a great *error*, not because of his depravity. These views have been elaborated, and abused. Aristotle would not have approved of unthinking adherence to his remarks on tragedy or on any subject, especially not in circumstances unlike those he knew. The best modern pupils of the Greek thinkers have been those who were willing to disagree with them. Since the rediscovery of his works in the Middle Ages, Aristotle has remained, despite doctrinaire followers and (sometimes hostile) critics, a fact of intellectual life.

In the fifth century Athens fought off the navy and armies of Persia and dominated Greece. In the fourth century Athens declined: Philip and his son Alexander the Great who were bitterly attacked in Athens by the orator Demosthenes (c.383–322BC), established a kingdom, and an empire which Alexander (356–323BC) extended to India. Alexander died young. His city Alexandria (in Egypt) came to succeed Athens as the centre of Greek culture. With the rise of Roman rule there were two literary languages in the Mediterranean region: Greek and Latin.

Many English poets have known Greek; most have known Latin, and most have read Virgil (or Vergil). Publius Vergilius Maro (70–19BC), who came from the village of Mantua, was the imperial poet of Rome under its first emperor Augustus (63BC–AD14). His epic *The Aeneid* was composed in conditions remote from the society and oral tradition of Homer, whom it imitates; it is 'literary epic'. Virgil tells the story of Aeneas, who links the histories of Troy and Rome. His theme is the destiny of Rome to rule and give laws to the world. The narrative begins in the middle of the story with Aeneas's journey from Troy to Carthage in North Africa; here Aeneas tells Queen Dido how Troy was taken. The love-affair between Dido and Aeneas, which ends with her suicide when he is obliged to continue his mission (told in Book IV), is perhaps the best part of the poem for a beginner who wishes to read a little. In Book VI Aeneas visits the Underworld and learns of Rome's future. In the remainder of the poem he fights wars in Italy, defeating Turnus. From this Trojan hero, says Virgil, Augustus is descended.

Virgil's influence on English writers has been long and pervasive. The English epic *Paradise Lost* (first edition 1667) by John Milton (1608–74) is shaped on Virgil's model in structure and, in many ways, in style. Virgil's *Eclogues* influenced pastoral poetry in English. His style, stately and haunting, is hard to imitate in English because the word order of Latin is far more free and because Latin poetry is quantitative, varying long and short syllables, while English verse depends on stressed syllables. But many poets have tried. Alfred Tennyson (1809-92) in his lines 'To Virgil' (published 1889) expresses, and faintly echoes, what has been admired in Virgil's work. The poem ends:

I salute thee Mantovano [Mantuan],
I that loved thee since my day began,
Wielder of the mightiest measure
Ever moulded by the lips of man.

Some Greek literature has influenced English writers through the Latin. The Greek dramatist Menander (c.342-292BC) wrote a 'New Comedy', based on everyday life. His work was lost (until one play was discovered in the twentieth century), but imitations by the Roman playwrights Plautus (c.254-184BC) and Terence (c.190-159BC) influenced English comedy. Shakespeare's *Comedy of Errors* (1594) was inspired by Plautus's *Menaechmi* where errors also arise from the confusing of twin brothers. The Latin *Metamorphoses* of Ovid (43BC-AD18) has made Greek mythology known to English writers since the Middle Ages.

Some of the best English lyrics of the Renaissance are imitations or free translations of Latin poems by Catullus (c.84-c.54BC) and Horace (65-8BC). The famous song in the play *Volpone* (1606) by Ben Jonson (1572-1637), 'Come my Celia, let us prove/While we can, the sports of love', is modelled on a poem by Catullus. Verse satire in the eighteenth century, especially in the work of Alexander Pope (1688-1744), was influenced by the satires of Horace and by the more 'savage' Roman satirist Juvenal (c.AD60-c.130).

It would be easy to enlarge and continue, and you should do so. Any English-language library or bookshop contains lively translations, in the Penguin Classics Series among others.* A good policy is to browse: to use spare moments to read a little, whenever possible; and to read at length, when you find an author who appeals to you. Read what you like – these are not set-texts. They will help you to discuss set-texts. Go back later to an author you find difficult at first. Translations are no substitute for the original but most of us need them; they have been used for centuries. The large sale of Alexander Pope's translations of Homer in the eighteenth century indicates the need for English versions among educated readers at a time when the ancient languages were rigorously taught (to boys). We have better and more easily available translations today than ever before.

---

*Penguin Books, Harmondsworth. For more details of recommended texts, see Part 5.

Introduction to English literary history

English studies often begin with Geoffrey Chaucer (*c.*1340-1400). It is helpful to know something about the six centuries of English literature before Chaucer. Ignorance has caused writers in later periods to disparage the Middle Ages as a 'dark' and 'barbarous' time; and alternatively to romanticise what seemed exotic. You should have certain facts clear: about the development of English as a literary language; about the role of the Church in early English culture; and about the main bearings of medieval writing.

The English language in the Middle Ages

English came to Britain in the fifth century following the end of the Roman occupation. As the Romans left, the Romanised Britons introduced mercenary troops from Germany and Denmark to protect them against marauders. Various peoples came in large numbers: Jutes, Angles and Saxons. They stayed, and by the end of the sixth century the newcomers had conquered England. Their Germanic language is known as Old English; it was very little affected by the Celtic of the Britons who were driven back into Wales and Cornwall, but took many loan-words from the Scandinavian Old Norse of the Viking invaders who attacked and partly settled the country in the ninth and tenth centuries. 'Heaven' is Old English; 'sky' is Norse.

The English warrior-nobles brought with them an oral tradition not unlike Homer's, with an elaborate poetic diction. The Old English of the epic *Beowulf* looks at first sight like a foreign language. When the hero announces himself, 'Beowulf is min nama!', we understand him; but the modern reader needs a translation for most of the poem. Works which are closer to the everyday speech of the time are easier to read. The best way to form your own impression is to compare a passage from the Old English translation of the Bible with the Authorised Version of 1611. There is a pleasure in seeing how far the word-order and rhythms of English have remained constant.

After the conquest of England by William of Normandy in 1066 the new ruling class spoke a northern dialect of French. Latin was the language of the Church and of much administration. Relatively little was written in English between the eleventh and the thirteenth centuries, although a few fine poems survive. In this period, when English was the spoken language of the (mostly illiterate) common people, the grammatical gender-forms (masculine, feminine, neuter) of Old English disappeared, and the system of case endings for nouns and adjectives was simplified: the *-s* ending for genitive singular and plural forms was all that survived, except in pronouns, and a few nouns (child*ren*, ox*en*). The 'weak' (*-ed*) ending in verbs (*play*, *played*) became standard, although some Old English 'strong' verbs survived (*sing, sang, sung*). Middle English came into being.

By the fourteenth century the French used in England was conspicuously different from that of France. A new sense of national identity in the upper classes gradually led to their adoption of English. Middle English acquired thousands of French (and Latin) loan-words in the process. French *mutton* was added to English *sheep*; French *pork* to English *pig*. French had little influence grammatically; but vocabulary was enriched. Consider this sentence: 'They danced to chamber-music around the table.' *Dance, chamber, music* and *table* are borrowings from French (*music* from French and Latin). The connecting words and the grammar are Old English. A few eccentric authors in the nineteenth century tried to write 'purely' by using only words of English extraction. Such a notion of purity is perverse. For seven centuries English writers have been able to choose among words close in meaning but subtly different. We have kept, for example, the Germanic habit of forming compounds: *bookman, word-list, foreword*. But we have alternative options: *scholar, glossary, preface*. Late Middle English was increased in scope; literature has benefited ever since.

English has always had dialects. Geoffrey Chaucer (c.1340–1400) wrote in the Middle English of London. William Caxton (1421–91), who introduced printing from the continent in 1476 made this the standard variety by printing it. Shakespeare introduced the phrase 'the king's English' (in *The Merry Wives of Windsor*, I.iv.5). Modern English, which we date from the early sixteenth century, has been dominated, especially in literary usage, by a development of the old dialect of the South East, although snobbish ideas in Britain about its social and cultural superiority mostly date from the later nineteenth century and have weakened in the last twenty years. Other varieties of English were spoken by emigrants, and flourish today among their descendants overseas.

The medieval Church

A Roman monk called Augustine converted King Ethelbert of Kent to Christianity in 596. Christianity was already established among the British; it spread quickly in England: with the new religion came literacy in English and Latin.

Anglo-Saxon paganism had been based on a stern code. Within the military caste absolute loyalty to the leader was the highest virtue; the best death was in battle. Dead warriors would feast in the *Valhalla* until the last, losing battle of men and gods against the dragon which gnaws at the world-tree *Yggdrasil*. Loyalty to kin was recognised by all. A slain kinsman had to be avenged, or his death compensated by blood-money.

Christianity made slow progress in affecting this system of values. *Beowulf*, which probably survives only because a monk wrote it down, has Christian insertions; its spirit is pagan. Epic style was used to produce poems on biblical and devotional subjects. A poem on the Fall of the Angels (known as 'Genesis B') may have influenced Milton's *Paradise Lost*. In the *Vision of the Cross*, one of the best short poems in Old English, Christ is presented as a young warrior to whom allegiance is due. In saints' lives and in sermons such Churchmen as Bishop Wulfstan (*d*.1023) and Aelfric (*d. c.*1020) attempted to Christianise the older culture. But in *The Battle of Maldon*, a tenth-century poem, we see that the military creed persisted. Alfred (849–901), King of the West Saxons, is an example of a soldier who served the Church by writing; he made several translations including an English version of the Latin *Ecclesiastical History* by the northern scholar Bede (673–735).

We owe Old English literature to the Church, and likewise much of Middle English writing was produced or preserved by clerics. *Clerk*, the medieval term for a clergyman, meant almost the same as *scholar* or *writer*. Priests used Latin in church, school and university affairs. After the eleventh century they would speak French in dealings with the upper class. They needed English in order to preach and guide their parishioners. They composed English carols and religious lyrics, and lyrics on other themes. The twelfth-century *Owl and the Nightingale* is a debate between the merits of religious and secular poetry.

The medieval drama may have developed out of songs used in church services. In the Miracle Plays, which began in the thirteenth century, everyday life is portrayed for a religious purpose. These were cycles of plays staged at town festivals. Stories from the Bible were adapted into a series of dramatic sketches, each presented (often on wagons) by a guild of workmen. A day's performances might begin with the Creation, continue with the stories of Adam and Eve, Noah and the Flood, Abraham and Isaac, and end with scenes from the life of Christ, his resurrection, 'harrowing' of Hell (a favourite subject), and ascent into Heaven. The roles of prophets, saints, devils, Christ, Mary, and God the Father were acted by townsmen. The language and settings were English and medieval. Comedy was included even for solemn occasions. Devils were comic. Noah is a comic figure, scolded by his wife. The shepherds in a Nativity Play from the cycle performed at Wakefield discover a stolen sheep hidden in a cradle, and toss Mak, the sheep-stealer, in a blanket before they are summoned by the angel to Christ's cradle in the manger. The purpose of the Churchmen who wrote the plays was to make these sacred stories real to the people; the result was the beginning of English drama.

The organisation of the Miracle cycles reflects the medieval Church's view of the Bible. Christian meanings were found throughout the Old

Testament. Old and New Testament stories were seen in 'typological' connection: in this view Abraham's willingness to sacrifice his son Isaac is a type or prefiguring of Christ's sacrifice. Eve's eating of the apple from the tree of knowledge causes the fall of man; Mary gives birth to man's redeemer. Humanity is preserved in Noah's ark and saved from sin by Christ's death so that the wood of the ark is compared to the wood of the cross. Correspondences of this sort were shown in the windows and sculptures of churches. They were used in poetry.

Christian meanings were also found in Latin authors. Virgil's fourth *Eclogue*, for example, which announces the birth of a child who will restore happiness to mankind, was seen as a prophecy of Christ's birth, and Virgil was revered. Ovid was a popular Latin poet often quoted as an 'authority'. Medieval argument was based on citations from earlier writers whose authority carried weight. A pleasant literary example from the late fourteenth century can be seen in 'The Nun's Priest's Tale', in Chaucer's *The Canterbury Tales*, where the cock Chanticleer argues with his wife about the interpretation of dreams. Boethius (d. AD525), the late Latin author of *On the Consolation of Philosophy*, was admired as a principal authority throughout the Middle Ages; he seemed to have reconciled ancient philosophy and Christianity. Boethius's image of Fortune's wheel occurs in many medieval poems. Fortune, under God, rules the affairs of men. The ancient art of astrology, it was believed, was a means of discovering how they were to change. What was known of ancient culture tended to be absorbed into a Catholic view of life.

There were intellectual dissidents within the Church. Roger Bacon (*c*.1214–94), a friar and scientific thinker, objected to the methods of *scholasticism* (arguing from principles derived from authorities); William Ockham (*d. c*.1349) also maintained that laws of knowledge must be based on the study of the natural world; both were accused of heresy. Although the Church stimulated intellectual and literary life, it was often repressive. Clerical influence induced Chaucer to repent of the more worldly of his Canterbury tales.

The Church provoked some writers to satire, especially in the fourteenth century. The friars and ecclesiastical officers were at worst corrupt. *The Canterbury Tales* includes satirical portraits of a 'Pardoner' who sells pardons and false relics to the credulous, and a 'Summoner' (or church-court official) who uses his position to extort money. The fourteenth-century poem *Piers Plowman*, attributed to William Langland (*c*.1330–*c*.1400), also attacks religious abuses. John Wycliffe (*c*.1230–84) attacked the Papacy and urged that people study the Bible for themselves. Such views were to lead in time to the Reformation.

Courtly and popular literature

Romance was the genre of courts. The favourite court of the romance-writers was Arthur's. Geoffrey of Monmouth (*d.*1154), an imaginative historian, wrote a full account of this legendary British king: Arthur comes to the throne in boyhood; he has a magic sword, Excalibur (there are various versions of the names in Arthurian (Celtic) legends); he becomes a conqueror. While he is on a journey to Rome he learns that his nephew Modred has usurped him and taken his wife Guenevere. Arthur returns; he kills Modred in a battle in Cornwall, but is badly wounded. Apparently dying, he is taken to the isle of Avalon. Other motifs, such as the round table where the knights sit as equals at Arthur's court in Caerleon, were added in later accounts.

Chrétien de Troyes, who lived in northern France in the later twelfth century, brought the conventions of courtly love to Arthurian romance. Courtly love was an aristocratic convention celebrated by the troubadours or court singers of Provence in the south of France. A humble suitor devotes himself to an idealised and haughty lady (not his wife); he will suffer anything in her service. In Chrétien the principles of ideal service and dedication are treated more seriously. The same virtues can be seen in an anonymous English romance of the fourteenth century: *Sir Gawain and The Green Knight*.

Gawain is at Arthur's court at Christmas when a great knight in green (the faery colour) arrives and issues a challenge. He and Gawain are to exchange blows with an axe. Gawain beheads the knight, who picks up his own severed head and orders the next meeting in a year's time, at the Green Chapel in the north. On his journey there Gawain stays at a castle. He and the lord of the castle agree to exchange winnings. The lord goes hunting and his lady tempts Gawain, three times. He resists. Twice she kisses him and he kisses her lord in return; then she gives him a magic girdle to make him invulnerable, and he keeps it. At the Green Chapel the green knight deals him two harmless blows with the axe, and one slight wound. The green knight is the lord of the castle, and the wound is to punish Gawain for keeping the girdle. His virtue has saved his head. None the less, Gawain is overcome by remorse at his failure in perfect honour. In Arthur's court he is laughed at as a perfectionist, and all agree to wear green girdles for his sake.

Moral scruple in a high-minded man who is only human is shrewdly observed in this romance. The alliterative technique, derived ultimately from Old English poetry, does not hamper the convincing dialogue. We enjoy the magic; we take the characters seriously. This is courtly literature at its most artful and intelligent.

Gawain is the best of knights. Other Arthurian heroes are less pure. Sir Launcelot's love for Guenevere leads to Arthur's downfall in *Le*

Morte Darthur by Thomas Malory (*d*.1471); Launcelot's sins prevent him from succeeding in his quest for the Holy Grail – the Cup of Christ's blood, in medieval tradition. Akin to the story of Launcelot and Guenevere is that of Tristram who marries Iseult of the White Hand, a Breton lady, but loves Iseult of Ireland, the wife of King Mark of Cornwall. Tristram too was eventually incorporated into the Arthurian legend.

The other major legend of the Middle Ages is set in Troy. Troilus and Cressida are medieval lovers, not part of the ancient story of the Trojan War. In Chaucer's *Troylus and Cryseyde* (1372–86) Troilus's passion affects him in a way that the Greeks would have found incomprehensible. He weeps; he cannot eat or fight. Cressida's uncle Pandarus unites the couple but Cressida is sent to the Greek camp where she betrays Troilus by taking the Greek Diomede as a lover. Troilus is eventually killed in battle by Achilles. Chaucer calls his poem a tragedy, and by this he means a pitiful story of ill-fortune. The pity and terror of Greek and Shakespearean tragedy are outside the scope of medieval writers. To them destiny is accomplished for the soul after death, and hell is the truly terrifying prospect. The pathos of *Troylus and Cryseyde* is blended with comedy. Troilus's idealistic, courtly passion is contrasted with the entertainingly practical realism of Pandarus.

Chaucer was a court poet, a scholar and intellectual. He translated at least part of *The Romaunt of The Rose* from a French allegorical poem of the early twelfth century and used its fashionable, learned but artificial conventions of dream-allegory in poems of his own. But he was always a realist. In *The Canterbury Tales*, composed between 1387 and 1400, he achieved the finest medieval synthesis of courtly and popular, 'high' and 'low' styles.

The tales show Chaucer's knowledge of French, Italian and Latin literature (he had visited France and Italy as a diplomat) and his knowledge of all levels of English social life. The Prologue is a series of portraits of pilgrims who set out from London for Canterbury; they tell stories to ease their journey and this gives Chaucer a framework for his (unfinished) collection. Some are romances or 'gentle' stories but many are polished performances in popular genres. 'The Miller's Tale' is a *fabliau*: a neatly plotted story of ordinary life, satirical, very funny, and for some readers (as Chaucer admits) improper. An Oxford student schemes to spend the night with the lovely young wife of his elderly landlord. He succeeds, but when he tries to be too clever in putting down a rival, he suffers for it. 'The Nun's Priest's Tale' is a fable inspired by the French tradition of popular, satirical animal stories featuring Reynard the Fox. 'The Prioress's Tale' is a sentimental, devotional piece, which illustrates various common prejudices. Chaucer made art from these materials and wrote for educated readers. Behind such tales were the conventions of story-telling belonging to people whose lives were remote from courts and courtly ideals.

Excellent contemporary-English versions of Chaucer by Neville Coghill are available in Penguin Classics: these make a pleasant introduction to medieval literature for non-specialists. Miracle plays (in modernised texts) are frequently performed at festivals and at universities in England. For those willing to attempt Middle English, lyrics and carols probably offer the best introduction. (For recommended editions, see Part 5.)

From the Renaissance to the Restoration

The sixteenth and seventeenth centuries form an exciting, and a complex, divided period. Most writers were strongly committed to religious, political, academic, or literary beliefs. The following outline is intended for students who are beginning to read Renaissance authors and for others who perhaps study only Shakespeare and later literature. Students of Keats will soon hear of Spenser and Milton; students of T. S. Eliot will hear of the metaphysicals. Knowledge of such terms as Christian humanism, Puritanism, and of course 'the Renaissance' are essential for an understanding of the tradition to which all later English writers belong.

Medieval civilisation had fixed boundaries: those of Europe and Christianity. Renaissance Europe was open to influences from other continents, including the newly-discovered Americas. There was a new sense of the past as another foreign country, different and worth knowing.

The medieval Church tried to assimilate Latin authors, and Aristotle whose work was known from the twelfth century. Dante Alighieri (1265–1321) was influenced by Aristotle and by Virgil. In Dante's *The Divine Comedy* there is a profound understanding of life but it is a medieval understanding. Two later Italian writers who learned from Dante – Petrarch (Francesco Petrarca; 1304–74) and Giovanni Boccaccio (1313–75) – became known as 'humanists': students of Greek and Latin culture as a source of new values. Under the patronage of such rich, independent families as the Medici of Florence in the fifteenth century, Greek manuscripts were collected, and writers and artists inspired by ancient civilisation were sheltered and encouraged. It was assumed that a humanist would be interested in all kinds of knowledge. Leonardo da Vinci (1452–1519) was a painter, sculptor, engineer, physicist, anatomist and writer. The range of his talents was exceptional, but not the range of his curiosity. The new learning led to inventions. Johann Gutenberg (*c*.1400–*c*.1468) invented printing with movable type and in the first century of printed books, humanist ideas spread across Europe, outside the direct control of the Church.

The English Renaissance came later than the Italian and was in many ways different. The fifteenth century was a troubled period of civil war in England. The arrival of the Dutchman Desiderius Erasmus (1466-1536), who lectured on Greek at Cambridge between 1511 and 1514, introduced humanist ideas from the continent. Erasmus's collection of ancient proverbs, the *Adagia* (1500), was widely influential. Sir Thomas More (1478-1535), a friend of Erasmus, published his Latin *Utopia* (Nowhere) in 1516. Communism, universal education and religious tolerance are practised in Utopia. The book was translated into many languages.

Some Englishmen were more concerned with the views of Martin Luther (1483-1546). Luther formed a Protestant League in Germany, and attacked abuses in the Catholic Church; he advanced the principle that an individual, studying the Bible for himself, should not be subject to Church authority in judging it. Private faith rather than submission to the doctrine and rites of the Catholic Church inspired Luther and the northern European Reformation. The Reformation reached England when King Henry VIII (reigned 1509-47) broke off relations with the Papacy over a problem of divorce. Thomas Cranmer (1489-1556) became Archbishop of Canterbury in 1533, recognising Henry as head of the English Church. Cranmer was burnt to death for heresy under the Catholic Queen Mary (reigned 1553-8) in 1556. Under Queen Elizabeth (reigned 1558-1603) a compromise was achieved within the Protestant Church of England between Catholic doctrine and the ideals of Puritan reformers. The Puritans were dissatisfied. Adopting an austere faith based strictly on the Bible, they were to be at worst narrowly intolerant of humanist culture, opposing the theatre in the time of Shakespeare; at best, they and other devout Protestants were able to achieve a form of Christian humanism.

The English Renaissance developed against this background of violent religious dispute. Italy, influential in literature, was disparaged by the English as immoral, and Catholic. But although the Reformation was a break with medieval Catholicism, many features of the older culture persisted. English Renaissance writers often remind us of medieval literature. *The Faerie Queene* (1589, 1596), a long, unfinished poem by Edmund Spenser (1552-99), is a Renaissance work, influenced by Italian poetry and ideas, which remains very English and in some ways old-fashioned. Spenser used Middle English archaisms; he drew on medieval romance for his story and on the medieval devices of allegory and personification for his method. The poem celebrates such international humanist ideals as that of the perfect gentleman, who was the subject of *The Courtier* (1528) by the Italian Baldassare Castiglione

(1478–1529). It also celebrates Queen Elizabeth and the Church of England.

William Shakespeare (1564–1616) grew up in a period of exceptional talent and originality. The first of his own gifts was the power to learn from others. In tragedy he learned from Christopher Marlowe (1564–93) and in comedy from John Lyly (1554–1606). Marlowe's *Tamburlaine The Great* (*c*.1587), *Doctor Faustus* (*c*.1588) and *Edward II* (*c*.1593) are tragedies which arise from character, from minds obsessed with power or knowledge or love. Marlowe made versatile, imaginative use of blank verse. Lyly wrote witty, mannered, erudite, poetical farces. Shakespeare followed their examples in developing structure from Latin models: Plautus in comedy, and Seneca (*d*. AD65) in tragedy. His literary inspiration came from many other sources, including Italian romances, which encouraged the romantic spirit of his comedies, and works on English and ancient history.

Various humanist ideas which filtered into English culture from Italy affected Shakespeare. Castiglione's concept of the Courtier impressed all Elizabethans. *The Prince* (1513) by Niccolo Machiavelli (1469–1527) was known at second hand. His principle of making immoral methods serve political purposes helped to shape such ruthless Shakespearean characters as Richard III. The French essayist Michel de Montaigne (1533–92) was known in England in translation. Montaigne is wise, sceptical, tolerant, opposed to pedantry, open-minded: he probably influenced Shakespeare's thought.

As a poet, in his sonnets and narrative poems and in the plays, Shakespeare adopted, and satirised, conventions of the time. Elizabethan poets took over the terminology and rhetoric of Petrarch's love poems. Exaggerated compliments and formulaic comparisons (often addressed to an idealised or imaginary lady) appear in Shakespeare, who liked but mocked them: 'my mistress' eyes are nothing like the sun' (Sonnet 130). 'Conceits', elaborate or ingenious images, were a taste of the time which Shakespeare shared. So were puns. English was still acquiring new words from Latin and French; these offered possibilities for a poet, and absurdities for a satirist. Shakespeare ridiculed what sounded pedantic or pretentious and (usually) adopted or invented what seemed natural to English.

There is also a medieval, English background to Shakespeare. The mixing of sublime poetry with coarse, grotesque and comic writing derives (in Shakespeare and in Spenser) from Middle English literature. It was to puzzle later classical critics. The miracle plays alternated high and low styles and scenes: the foolery of the shepherds and the birth of Christ. Sermons and lyrics did the same; and so did Chaucer. Medieval drama ranged widely in time and space, from God in heaven above the stage to the devils in hell below; from the Garden of Eden to the

Resurrection. Shakespeare ranges from Egypt to Rome and back again in *Antony and Cleopatra* (*c*.1606); from England to France in *Henry V* (1599); from Scotland to England and back in *Macbeth* (*c*.1606). The miracle cycles were suppressed by the Protestant Church, but their conventions survived. The allegorical morality plays, another branch of the old drama, may have influenced the design in some of Shakespeare's plays. Prince Hal is tempted from his duty by Falstaff in the two Parts of *Henry IV* (*c*.1597) rather as Youth in the moralities was tempted by the figure of Vice.

Any good writer alters the nature of a genre or tradition by writing in it. Many genres and traditions – classical, Renaissance and medieval – met in Shakespeare's work and he transformed them all. The same can be said of the chief poet of the mid-seventeenth century, Milton.

The life and work of John Milton (1608–74) illustrates how humanist learning and literary ambition could be combined with commitment to the cause of Protestantism in the English Late Renaissance. Milton was a tireless student. At Cambridge and afterwards (1632–7) in private study at home he made himself formidably well-read in English, Latin, Greek, Hebrew, and Italian. From 1637 to 1639 he travelled abroad visiting scholars, especially in Italy. As a poet he set himself to excel in a series of different genres: he wrote an ode 'On the Morning of Christ's Nativity' in 1621; a pair of idylls, 'L'Allegro' ('The Happy Man') and 'Il Penseroso' ('The Contemplative') in 1632; *Comus*, a masque, in 1634; and 'Lycidas', an elegy, in 1637. He planned his epic *Paradise Lost* (composed 1658–63; published 1667) to be a Christian, Protestant equivalent to Virgil's *Aeneid*; it is. Only in its sequel, the relatively disappointing *Paradise Regained* (1671) did his piety get the better of his talent. *Samson Agonistes* (1671) is a poetic drama in the manner of Greek tragedy. After the outbreak of the Civil War in 1642 Milton wrote on behalf of the Puritans. He defended the execution of Charles I (reigned 1625–49). He was Latin (Foreign) Secretary under the Puritan 'Commonwealth' of Oliver Cromwell (ruled 1653–8), continuing even when he became blind, until the Restoration of the monarchy in 1660 when he was arrested and fined. Milton was a scholar, a poet, a theologian, and a polemicist in state affairs. At no other period in England have these activities been so united. There is a strong urgency in everything Milton wrote, whether on Christian doctrine, the role of classical poetry in education, or social revolution. He was fortunate to survive the Restoration: in Europe at this time intellectuals were frequently executed for what they had written, for writing was seen as the exercise of power.

Paradise Lost was composed with the Renaissance ambition of competing with Virgil, and with a Protestant aim 'to justify the ways of God to man'. In structure it is modelled on the *Aeneid*; the long periods of its grand style look Latinate but close study has shown how true to English they are. Milton combines biblical material with classical myth; he makes the gods of ancient epic the fallen angels who rebel in vain against God and deceive mankind. Greek myth is a source of elaborate images and analogies: the Garden of Eden, for example, is compared to Enna in Sicily where Persephone (Proserpine) was carried off by Pluto (Dis):

> ... that fair field
> Of Enna where Proserpin gathering flowers,
> Herself a fairer flower, by gloomy Dis
> Was gathered ...
>
> (IV.268-71)

So Eve is to be gathered by Satan. Such beautiful but 'erring' legends are assimilated; they illustrate, Milton believes, the truth.

The poem's argument is that God has given man freedom to choose the truth. The danger to Christianity in the high-Protestant principle of free inquiry and discussion was that men would argue themselves out of believing. Milton thought that impossible if they followed 'right reason'. The devils in *Paradise Lost* argue forever and get nowhere because their reason is corrupted; but for men, Milton thought, the truth is inescapable. This conviction made him a liberal. In his prose *Areopagitica** (1644) he argues magnificently for freedom from censorship. He urges that the 'Lords and Commons of England' 'give me liberty to know, to utter, and to argue freely, according to conscience, above all liberties'. The English, Milton declares, are 'a nation not slow and dull, but of a quick, ingenious and piercing spirit'. It was a good claim.

Religious poetry and prose was written with intelligence, learning and argumentativeness throughout Milton's lifetime. John Donne (1571-1631) was the leader of the 'metaphysical' poets, who combined strong feeling with learned ingenuity, in rebellion against the conventional imagery of Elizabethan love-poems. They took images from philosophy, logic, mathematics, astronomy, history and legend, and drew daring comparisons. Donne was an *avant-garde* intellectual who became a passionate believer. He turned from love-poems to dramatic and personal religious poems. The sermons he wrote as Dean of St Paul's Cathedral in London include some of the best prose of the time. (The sermon was a lively and popular genre in the seventeenth century.) Ben Jonson (1572-1637), a scholar and the best playwright of his time after Shakespeare, was a court-poet, writing with deliberate grace, rather than with the clever roughness of the metaphysicals. He was a Christian humanist; he wrote masques – elaborate court entertainments – love-

*The Areopagus was a hill at Athens where the Upper Council met.

poems and lyrics, combining a love for classical literature with a sturdy, devout moral purpose.

George Herbert (1593-1633) wrote religious poems which are traditional in using the typological correspondences of the Middle Ages, but metaphysical in presenting them as daring 'conceits'. *Religio Medici* (A Doctor's Religion) by Sir Thomas Browne (1605-82), published in 1643, is a stylish, erudite prose confession of faith by a scientist with a very lively mind. Donne, Jonson, Herbert, and Browne are typical of their period and especially so in their individuality; like Milton and most Renaissance writers in England they were believers and spirited free thinkers.

Diversity of opinion in the mid-seventeenth century can be seen in a number of groups of thinkers, some of whom were politically radical: the egalitarian views of the 'Diggers' and 'Levellers' were not to emerge again until the nineteenth century. The 'Cambridge Platonists', who included Ralph Cudworth (1617-88) and Nathaniel Culverwel (*d. c.*1651), are often found attractive and interesting today. Platonic thought had permeated Renaissance literature. At Cambridge University this circle advanced a view of the spiritual nature of the universe to combat the more extreme forms of Puritanism and of non-Christian theories which were to find followers after the Restoration.

From the Restoration to the Romantics

The year 1660 was felt by those who celebrated the Restoration of the monarchy to mean a new start, and it did: in the theatre, in science, in politics, in prose-writing, in verse technique, and in the mood of the times. Many students feel at home in the period that followed. Science, journalism, satire, the novel – modern literature is starting to take shape. It is relatively easy for beginners to read widely for themselves. Philosophers and theorists, novelists, and poets are often more lucid and cogent than their twentieth-century successors. The danger in writing about Restoration and eighteenth-century literature is oversimplification. Such terms as 'the enlightenment', 'the neo-classical period' have a value, but not all authors subjected the heart to the head or cared about Latin. Many features of the Romantics can be seen in earlier work. Caution is required. (Caution as a rule for examinees is discussed in Part 4.)

The Restoration of the monarchy under King Charles II, who reigned from 1660 to 1685, enabled the London theatres, closed by the Puritans in 1642, to open in changed conditions. Women replaced the boy-actors who had previously taken female roles. Stages were framed as they are today and stage machinery was introduced. Plays were written for the courtiers who came back from exile in France with French ideas. Neo-classicism was taken seriously there; the dramatic 'unities' (derived from Aristotle) of one expanse of time, one setting, and one action, were respected. Ben Jonson, who had kept closer than Shakespeare to classical structure, was influential in the new drama. But the Restoration court was licentious to an extent the moralist Jonson would have disapproved. Charles and his favourite, the poet John Wilmot, Earl of Rochester (1648-80), were urbane sensualists; their court circle was in revolt against Puritan restraints. The respectable middle classes thought Restoration comedy grossly improper.

The Comical Revenge: or Love in a Tub (1664) by Sir John Etherege (1634-91) combined a serious plot with comedy, and rhymed verse with prose. Etherege influenced the later plays of William Wycherley (1614-1716), William Congreve (1670-1729), and others who wrote in prose and couplets. These are comedies of manners satirising social behaviour (as Jonson had done); certain types came to be expected: witty lovers, coquettes, rich widows, foolish country-gentlemen, lusty old husbands of young wives. Tricks, disguises, marital disputes and extra-marital pursuits, indulgently or (in Wycherley) scathingly treated, are cleverly managed and meant to make us laugh. Congreve's *The Way of the World* (1700) is the play to begin with. This mode of drama which outlasted Charles's reign, was ousted by Sir Richard Steele (1672-1729) in his comedies of 'sentiment' (in the eighteenth-century sense of moral precept), emphasising virtue. Steele's *The Conscious Lovers* (1722) includes a lecture against duelling. When Richard Brinsley Sheridan (1751-1816) revived the high-spirited satire of the Restoration, Steele's influence can be seen at its best: in its faith in good nature. Read Sheridan's *The School for Scandal* (1777).

John Dryden (1631-1700) wrote a series of heroic tragedies involving emperors and princesses in exotic settings, wars and passions, and very complicated plots. *Tyrannic Love: or The Royal Martyr* (1669) is a characteristic title. Dryden was the best poet of the Restoration and the plays contain good lyrics and verse passages, but also bombast. They were ridiculed effectively in *The Rehearsal* (1672) by the prominent courtier George Villiers, Duke of Buckingham (1628-87). Dryden wrote a moving blank-verse tragedy on the story of Antony and Cleopatra, *All for Love* (1678); but it is hard to do it justice if one knows Shakespeare's play. No one since Shakespeare's time has written a tragedy which will compare with the best work of his period. Eighteenth-century tragedies highly praised by contemporaries, such as *Cato* (1713) by Joseph Addison (1672-1719), are not admired today.

In 1662 Charles II granted a charter to the 'Royal Society' for the discussion of science and philosophy. The advance of science is one key to understanding the period. In southern Europe Catholic resistance to Protestantism (in a movement called the Counter-Reformation) had caused the imprisonment of scientists, including the astronomer Galileo Galilei (1564-1642) who defended, and was then forced to recant, the theory of Copernicus (Nicolas Koppernik; 1473-1543) that the earth and other planets move in orbit round the sun. England had been tolerant of free inquiry. The philosopher Francis Bacon (1561-1626) had argued for scientific study by inductive methods based on experience as a means for man to gain power over nature. The chemist Robert Boyle (1627-91) and the physicist Isaac Newton were members of the Royal Society. Newton's theories on light and colours, on the laws of motion, and on universal gravitation created the impression among many intellectuals that the secrets of Nature had been made clear. According to Alexander Pope (1688-1744) 'Nature and Nature's Laws lay hid in Night;/God said, Let Newton be! and all was light' ('Epitaph for Sir Isaac Newton').

The Royal Society included men of letters. John Dryden belonged. Dryden and others decided that English prose needed reforming. The best early seventeenth-century prose, as in the 1611 'Authorised' translation of the Bible which has influenced English writers ever since, is sonorous, resonant and impressive. Some prose-writers had been brief and pithy, using short sentences, as Bacon did. But others imitated the Roman rhetorician Cicero (106-43BC) and used very complex patterns of clauses. The aim of much Renaissance prose was to be persuasively eloquent. Rich diction, allusion and imagery were admired; they added to 'eloquence' which was an art all students learned. Milton is eloquent:

> I cannot praise a fugitive and cloistered virtue, unexercised and unbreathed, that never sallies out and sees her adversary, but slinks out of the race, where that immortal garland is to be run for, not without dust and heat.
>
> *(Areopagitica)*

Milton says that virtue should not be sheltered as though in a monastery but must fight against evil in gruelling trials in order to achieve salvation. That sentence is a poor substitute for Milton's; it would stir no one; but the meaning is more quickly grasped. Milton uses three metaphors: the virtue he cannot praise is that of an unhealthy, timid monk (in a cloister) who refuses to act as a warrior or as a runner in a hot dusty race for the prize of heaven. His sentence needs to be held in the mind as a whole, pondered, and enjoyed.

John Dryden and others wanted to make prose more functional, better suited to clear explanations in science or philosophy. Dryden wrote a lucid, plain, quickly readable prose, which was adopted by others. Jonathan Swift (1667-1745) in his satire *Gulliver's Travels* (1726) is plain and forceful:

> Whoever could make two ears of corn or two blades of grass to grow upon a spot of ground where only one grew before would deserve better of mankind and do more essential service to his country than the whole race of politicians put together.
>
> (Part 2, Chapter 7)

This is modern prose. Its invention made possible the development of the essay and of other forms of prose-writing, including the novel.

John Locke (1632-1704) published *An Essay Concerning Human Understanding* in 1690. This is a major work of philosophy, an 'essay' in the grandest sense. Locke founded analytical philosophy; he argued for tolerance to replace the fierce religious disputes of the Civil War; he wrote an essay on the 'Reasonableness of Christianity' (1695) arguing for faith on the grounds that we cannot fully understand reality. The religious debates of the sixteenth and seventeenth century concerned how to interpret Christianity. From the Restoration onwards the question of whether to believe in Christianity became increasingly pressing. Anthony Ashley Cooper, third Earl of Shaftesbury (1671-1713) was among those who preferred Deism: belief in a Supreme Being without commitment to Christian doctrine. Reasonableness was the theme of Joseph Addison and Richard Steele in their periodicals the *Tatler* (1709-11) and the *Spectator* (1711-12; 1714). A humane, tolerant sense of proportion was recommended in their quiet, polite essays. A balance had been achieved in the state so that monarchs, after the expulsion of James II (reigned 1685-8), were increasingly constitutional; political power, after the advent of Sir Robert Walpole (1676-1745) as Prime Minister (1721-42), was vested in Parliament. The great aristocratic families allied with the merchant class to form the Whig party, opposed by the gentry and by staunch Anglicans and royalists in the Tory Party. Political rivalry was hot and involved able satirists – Swift and Pope. But moderation and 'sense' were respected at least in principle.

The rise of the novel would not have been possible without the new prose, or without the existence of a large middle class with private leisure to be filled. Novelists faced opposition. *Robinson Crusoe* (1719) and *Moll Flanders* (1722) by Daniel Defoe (?1660-1731) seemed 'lies', because they adopted the form of factual narrative without the conspicuously artificial conventions of romance. Ordinary people became heroes and heroines; they had not had central roles in the plays of Shakespeare or in the romances. In *Pamela* (1740) by Samuel Richardson (1689-1761) the heroine is a servant-girl (although she becomes a lady). Another objection to novels was that women and servants would waste their time reading such works as *Pamela* and pick up wicked ideas (Pamela, for instance, marries her master). Another problem was that novels had no real antecedents in ancient literature. Henry Fielding (1707-54), who, unlike Defoe and Richardson, was classically educated, was troubled by this lack of literary respectability. In *Joseph Andrews* (1742) Fielding started out to parody *Pamela* and wrote an entertaining story (which makes a good introduction to eighteenth-century literature), full of humour and good sense. But here and in *Tom Jones* (1749) Fielding is haunted by memories of the classical epic which he parodies, conscious of the gap between heroic princes in Homer and Virgil and his humbler characters from everyday life. He thought of his novels as comic prose epics. To add weight he introduced essays on the part of the narrator; they are excellent but they interrupt the story. Fielding lacked confidence in the novel.

Despite their position as outsiders in literature the early novelists explored the possibilities of fiction with thoroughgoing intelligence. *Tristram Shandy* (1760-2; 1765; 1767) by Laurence Sterne (1713-68) plays with the makeup of fiction, its ordering of life and its illusory nature. He still fascinates theorists of the novel. Jane Austen (1775-1817) who had more respect than Sterne for order and illusion, wrote into the nineteenth century; she is the last of the early novelists. Her books, shapely, vivid, moral, and wittily ironic, are, for some readers, almost perfect.

Literary perfection of a kind was the object of many poets and was achieved by Alexander Pope. His *Essay on Criticism* (1711) offers a definition:

True wit is nature to advantage dress'd;
What oft was thought, but ne'er so well express'd.

Wit used to mean more than it does today: intelligence, good expression, learning, talent – and those who possess them, the *wits*. The idea of dressing nature to advantage reveals Pope's view of civilisation: elegant costume, formal gardens, fine artefacts, graceful phrasing were means to impose order, calm, and good taste. Pope's heroic couplet does so. Although Milton had chosen blank verse for *Paradise Lost*, Dryden and poets after the Restoration adopted rhymed pentameters as the most civilised verse form. Pope learned from Dryden. His couplets were suited to the social, theoretic, satirical, cerebral poetry he mostly wrote. The paired lines and the pause within a line create an effect of poise; his antitheses are memorable: (denouncing an enemy as Pope often did) 'Alive ridiculous, and dead forgot'. The danger was monotony but Pope subtly varied the structure of his lines and learned to compose verse paragraphs in couplets.

'Neo-classical' is a term applied to Pope and his contemporaries. Classical and especially Latin literature had never been more respected. Pope wrote 'Imitations' of Horace's *Satires* and attempted to give his verse the tight epigrammatic quality found in some Latin poets. The term 'Augustan' was applied by Pope and others, partly in mockery, to their own age, recalling the reign of the Roman Emperor when Horace and Virgil flourished. Pope can have a Roman pungency. His poem 'On the Characters of Women' notes: 'Most women have no characters at all.' In *The Rape of the Lock* (1712; 1714) Pope wrote a mock epic on the subject of an aristocratic quarrel: a young gentleman had cut off a lock of a lady's hair. When treated in the grand manner of heroic poetry the passions involved become pleasantly absurd: 'Not louder screams to pitying heaven are cast/When husbands or when lapdogs breathe their last.'

Some readers think Pope too facile and prefer Dryden's satires in heroic couplets (*Absalom and Achitophel*, 1681, a political poem in defence of Charles II, is the best). That is a matter of personal preference. Others think Pope trivial, artificial and malicious. *The Seasons* by James Thomson (1700–48), published in four Parts (1726–30), is very different: a nature poem in blank verse. The 'Song to David' (1763) by Christopher Smart (1722–71) is an original, startling hymn to King David, author of the Old Testament Psalms. Any good anthology of eighteenth-century verse is worth exploring. (See Part 5.)

Literature between the Restoration and the Romantics is intriguingly varied. Generalisations are hard to find; tendencies conflict. There are great works of scepticism and of belief. The political treatise *Leviathan* (published 1651 but properly a Restoration book) by Thomas Hobbes (1588–1679) sees man as a selfish being, naturally at war with others, having no innate regard for morals; morality and authority are means adopted by men to discipline themselves and make social life possible. *Leviathan*, written in cuttingly clear prose, must have been disconcerting to intelligent Christian readers. But the most successful of all religious works in English, *The Pilgrim's Progress* (1678, 1684) by John Bunyan (1628–88) might have consoled them. The pilgrim Christian travels from the City of Destruction to the Celestial City meeting allegorical obstacles and adversaries (The Slough of Despond; Mr Worldly Wiseman). He reaches his goal.

There are other discrepancies. Pope's (verse) *Essay on Man* (1732–4) attempts to argue away the problem of evil; all is for the best, if only we could see it. But Pope's friend Swift presents in the guise of a fantastic travel-book, *Gulliver's Travels*, a satire which strongly asserts the evil in man. Dr Samuel Johnson (1709–84) commented on the *Essay on Man* that 'never were penury of knowledge and vulgarity of sentiment so happily disguised'. The terms *sentiment*, *sentimentality*, and *sensibility* were associated with the feelings, with the heart rather than the head, and with moral goodness. Despite the respect for reason, a vogue for the sentimental developed in the eighteenth century. Laurence Sterne's *A Sentimental Journey* (1768), an account of travels in France and Italy,

Background to study · 51

represents sentimentality as an ability to sympathise with others even in the most trivial matters. Sentiment appears in the rise of the novel, and in popular revivals of religious enthusiasm, including the Methodist movement started by John Wesley (1703-91).

Dr Johnson was a complex man in many ways representative of his period: rough in manner and tender in feeling; pessimistic and afraid of death, yet a firm Christian; doctrinaire yet generously intelligent. His criticism is rooted in neo-classical rules about the need for dramatic unities and for purity of genre; but he recognised the quality of Shakespeare in spite of his own theories. As a critic and poet he believed (like most poets since Dryden) in rhyme, but admitted that Milton was right to use blank verse for *Paradise Lost*. Johnson's *Lives of the Poets* (1779-81) includes verdicts on poetry with which most modern readers disagree, but even when wrong-headed his criticism is worth disagreeing with; when judgements are right they are formidably well explained. Johnson was a poet, an essayist, a moralist, and the author of the first English dictionary (1755). He was a great talker on all subjects. His conversations were recorded by James Boswell (1740-95) in *The Life of Samuel Johnson* (1791). This is one of the best biographies in English, and a good book to have at hand for occasional browsing. The range and variety of Johnson's time appear in his talk.

Romanticism

The Romantic poets approached literature in a new spirit and with confidence. 'In a sense all poetry is Romantic,' wrote the German critic Friedrich von Schlegel (1772-1829). Medieval and Renaissance culture was enthusiastically reinterpreted by Romantic poets and writers in England and in Germany and France, in the late eighteenth and early nineteenth centuries: all works of the imagination were found to be good.

In Germany and France Romanticism was an abrupt new start. In France (in the 1820s and 1830s) it was a revolt against neo-classicism which had tried to find literary rules, derived from ancient literature, to match the laws of science. In England there was no abrupt revolt. Edward Young (1683-1765), a poet of 'sensibility', published *Conjectures on Original Composition* in 1759. He distinguished between imitation of classical models and originality or genius. An original, spontaneous work, he wrote, 'grows' of its own nature. Samuel Taylor Coleridge (1772-1834) was to develop this view in his theories of the creative *imagination* and of the organic (living) nature of an imaginative creation. In England poetry preceded theory. In the poetry of Young, Thomson, Smart, and William Blake (1757-1827), and in novels, there was a gradual departure from neo-classicism. Admiration of Shakespeare, whose plays had been distorted in neo-classical adaptations for the stage, mellowed dogmatism about rules and 'reason' because Shakespeare appeared to transcend both. Many German writers considered Shakespeare to have been the first Romantic.

The French philosopher Voltaire (François Marie Arouet, 1694–1778), who condemned Shakespeare's apparent disregard for rules of unity and purity of genre, wrote that he valued poetry only as an ornament to reason. That view was never quite accepted in England, and it was energetically contradicted by the Romantics who proclaimed the imagination – perhaps irrational and certainly unpredictable – as the highest faculty, and the mind as a richer and more mysterious blessing than Voltaire's 'reason'. Medieval and Renaissance culture was reappraised, imitated (and often misunderstood). The results of the new faith in imagination were so complex that any single definition of Romanticism is inadequate, especially in England where, with no 'school' of Romantics, every writer was his own man. In William Wordsworth (1770–1850) a reverence for nature's presence in a country childhood and moral influence in adult life was fostered by the poet's upbringing in the mountainous Lake District of north-west England, and by Coleridge's ideas. In Percy Bysshe Shelley (1792–1822) idealism, which was partly republican and liberal, partly mystical and Platonic, and entirely youthful, caused him to hope for the regeneration of mankind. Both looked beyond the real to the ideal, beyond the immediate to the transcendental. In the odes of John Keats (1795–1821), composed in 1819, there is a luxuriant, lyric blending of observed and imagined worlds. 'I describe what I imagine,' Keats wrote, in a letter to his brother George in September 1819. He did both well. Keats died at twenty-six; the English Romantic poets all did their best work while young; there is considerable confusion and nothing of a manifesto in their critical writings. Keats's observations on poetry come in his letters. Wordsworth and Coleridge published in 1800 a Preface to the second edition of their joint work, *Lyrical Ballads* (1798), defending poetry-in-plain-words. In his *Biographia Literaria* (1817) Coleridge records that Wordsworth took everyday things for his subject and Coleridge 'the supernatural or at least the romantic' (Chapter 14). The supernatural was linked with romance as a medieval genre, in Coleridge and in the Gothic novel: that is another strand in Romanticism. Lord Byron (George Gordon, 1788–1824) made his lively personality a Romantic inspiration throughout Europe. Like the dark, glamorous figures of his narrative poems, he rebelled, in his private life, against 'conventional morality'; he left England and died while fighting for Greek independence. But English Romanticism is full of contradictions: Byron attacked Wordsworth and Coleridge. His line 'thou shalt believe in Milton, Dryden, Pope' is from his best work, the epic satire *Don Juan*

(1819-24), a witty, sardonic social-comedy in verse.

One definite point is that these writers were versatile in metre and stanza form. They believed that each poem should be shaped to suit its own nature: poems should evolve. Wordsworth's *The Prelude* (1799-1805; first published 1851), a verse autobiography of the growth of the poet's mind, belongs to no genre. But Wordsworth, Shelley, and Keats wrote sonnets – one of the strictest verse-forms. Keats, Shelley and Byron invented stanza forms, but also wrote in *ottava rima* and in the Spenserian stanza. Coleridge's *The Ancient Mariner* (1798) is a ballad. No form was considered ideal, but any might be found appropriate for a particular poem. Every poem was a new venture.

Most later writers have been affected by the Romantic Movement. Novelists such as Emily Brontë (1818-48) and D. H. Lawrence (1885-1930) can be discussed as Romantics. Although realism (the business of most novelists) is sometimes said to be the 'opposite' of Romanticism, social and psychological realism can never be independent of an individual novelist's personality and imagination. In symbolism, in concern with childhood, with nature, with all inner-life, and with the poetry of the commonplace, novels have always been influenced by Romanticism.

Some writers have seen the Romantic Movement as a regeneration of literature; others have seen it as a disastrous breakdown of order and values. It is generally agreed that Romanticism created the conditions from which modern culture has emerged.

Many twentieth-century writers have attempted to rebel. T. S. Eliot (1888-1965) called himself a 'classical' poet and critic. He revived interest in metaphysical poetry and in Pope. W. B. Yeats (1865-1939) wrote in a Romantic, symbolist manner in the 1890s, but his later work gained in dramatic and realistic quality. He drew on Irish legend and history in his poems, and in his poetic drama. 'Things fall apart, the centre cannot hold,' wrote Yeats in 'The Second Coming' (1921): 'Mere anarchy is loosed upon the world.' He expected an end to the present historical cycle and the birth of a new era. D. H. Lawrence considered modern life to be corrupted by industrialism and 'close to an end'. Such attitudes are partly attributable to the failure of Romantic ideals, although the earliest Romantic writers tended to veer between extremes of optimism and despair at the state of the world. Since the end of the eighteenth century there has been no shared, integrated, coherent view of life in European civilisation. Several distinct sets of beliefs coexist in modern minds. That has been both stimulating and disturbing.

Any modern work you study can be seen in relation to the continuous tradition of literature in English; indeed it cannot be divorced from its whole background, which goes back a long way. Classical allusions or references to Renaissance writers in a good contemporary poem, novel, or play are not affectations but symptoms of the writer's dependence on past literature. Understanding ourselves involves looking backwards. If you can come to see your set-books in their full context you will enjoy them more and write about them much more effectively. Parts 3 and 4 take examples chiefly from Shakespeare and from nineteenth- and twentieth-century writers who have only been touched on in this section. The aim in this introduction to English literary history has been to indicate the connections which link separate periods and various individual talents.

Glossary of literary terms

The following terms occur frequently in criticism and literary history. Terms are in italics when further information is supplied in other entries.

acrostic: a poem in which the first letters in a series of lines form a pattern or a word

aestheticism: the view that literature (and art in general) has no moral or social purpose and that pleasure in the beauty of form, or in wit, is all that matters. The Aesthetic Movement of the late nineteenth century was marked by the extravagant dandyism of its followers, who included Oscar Wilde (1854–1900)

Alexandrine: an iambic line of six feet

allegory: an extended metaphor; a narrative in which characters, places and other details have figurative meanings. In Edmund Spenser's *The Faerie Queene* the Red Crosse Knight of Holiness stands for the Anglican Church; he protects the virgin Una, who stands for true religion

alliteration: deliberate repetition of a letter or sound especially at the beginning of words: 'five *m*iles *m*eandering with a *m*azy *m*otion'. Old English and some Middle English poetry relied on a strict scheme of alliteration

ambiguity: (i) a failure in clarity where the meaning is carelessly left unclear; (ii) a deliberate, creative mixture of meanings or feelings, especially in poetry

anachronism: attribution to one historical period of what belongs to another

analogue: similar ideas, themes or stories occurring independently in two or more writers or cultures are analogues. Not to be confused with a source

anapaest:	see *foot*
anti-novel:	see *nouveau roman*
antithesis:	the arrangement of phrases or clauses to emphasise contrast: 'He for God only: she for God in him'
aphorism:	a pithy statement of some general truth: 'art is long; life is short'
Apollonian:	a mode of literature in which reason and order prevail; its counterpart is *Dionysian*
archaism:	the use of words no longer in current use
archetype:	(i) the earliest form of an institution or phenomenon; (ii) an image or idea in the collective subconscious; (iii) a term used vaguely of anything felt to be universal or deeply rooted in human life
argument:	(i) the summary of a work as a prologue or marginal note; (ii) a main theme or purpose
assonance:	the rhyming of vowels
asyndeton:	the omission of connecting words: 'I came, I saw, I conquered'
axiom:	a self-evident truth
ballad:	originally a song for dancers. Late medieval narrative poems of oral origin, in short stanzas, are known as ballads. Some Romantic poets imitated their method and stanza form:

> O Wedding Guest! This soul hath been
> Alone on a wide wide sea;
> So lonely 'twas that God himself
> Scarce seeméd there to be.
> (S. T. Coleridge, 'The Rime of the Ancient Mariner', 1798)

ballade:	an intricate old French form of poetry imitated by nineteenth-century poets. The three stanzas are of equal length (often eight lines) and end with a refrain and a four line 'envoy'; the rhyme scheme is regular; the same line ends each stanza and envoy
baroque; rococo:	architectural terms sometimes (rather vaguely) applied to seventeenth-century poetry possessing ornate, luxuriant design and patterning
bathos:	unintentional anti-climax
bildungsroman:	(*German*) a novel dealing with its hero's early years and education
blank verse:	unrhymed iambic pentameters (see *metre*), used by Marlowe, Shakespeare, Milton and many later poets

bowdlerise: to edit out words or passages felt to be improper. Dr Thomas Bowdler (1774–1825) published an expurgated *Family Shakespeare* in 1818

burlesque: from Italian *burla*, 'mockery'; to ridicule by exaggeration; a work which mocks the conventions of another

caesura: a break, and so a pause, within a line of verse

caricature: a style of drawing or writing which exaggerates the peculiar features of a character or group of characters

catastrophe: the outcome of a story or play, not necessarily unhappy; the final act, or denouement

catharsis: according to Aristotle, the emotional purifying of an audience through the pity and terror aroused by tragedy

cavalier: a mode of *courtly* lyric poetry

chiasmus: the crossing of phrases in a parallel construction: 'to live is wearisome; it is terrible to die'

chorus: in Greek drama the chorus witnessed the action and commented in song. Milton used a chorus in *Samson Agonistes*

chronicle: an historical account of events year by year, as in the *Anglo-Saxon Chronicle* in Old English. Nineteenth-century novelists sometimes used the term whimsically of their own work

chronicle-plays: Elizabethan history-plays presenting a loose sequence of events

Ciceronian: prose modelled on the Latin style of Cicero with complex elaborate sentence-structure

circumlocution: or periphrasis; a roundabout, indirect form of expression

classic(al): adjective used to describe (i) a recognised masterpiece; (ii) ancient Latin or Greek literature; (iii) writing influenced by ancient models. See *neo-classicism* and *Romanticism*

cliché: an expression that has lost its originality through over-use

climax: (i) the build-up to a high-point in rhetoric; (ii) the high or low point in dramatic development; the third act in a play of five acts

comedy: a light, amusing form of drama ending happily, with marriages and reconciliations. Sentimental comedy in the eighteenth century emphasised good nature and morality, in reaction to the caustic amorality of

Restoration comedy. Comedy of Manners deals with social behaviour. See *burlesque*, *farce*, *humours*, and *tragi-comedy*

commitment: any sincere writer can be 'committed', but the term is used especially for those who use literature for political or social purposes

complication: the second of five acts in a play

conceit: (i) in Elizabethan poetry a simile, metaphor, or extended figure of speech; (ii) in metaphysical poetry, an ingenious, surprising use of figurative language

couplet: two rhyming lines of verse

courtly: Ben Jonson and his imitators in the early seventeenth century wrote a 'courtly' lyric poetry, concerned with love and honour, clear and elegant in style

courtly love: perhaps of Arabic origin, the aristocratic conventions of courtly love travelled north from Provence in southern France in the twelfth century. The courtly lover is the humble, pure, honourable, and patient servant of a haughty lady

dactyl: see *foot*

decadence: a development of Romanticism celebrating the beauty of the horrible, of pain and death, and of forbidden pleasures

denouement: (*French*) see *catastrophe*

deus ex machina: (*Latin*) the god from the 'machine'; in ancient drama the gods might descend from a raised platform, or 'machine', and intervene in human affairs on the stage below. The device is used in English plays and masques, including *The Tempest*

diction: the selection and arrangements of words in a work of literature; see *poetic diction*

didactic(ism): didactic writing aims to instruct

digression: a temporary departure from the main theme or story

Dionysian: a mode of literature in which the emotional, irrational and Romantic prevail; its counterpart is *Apollonian*

discourse: a term borrowed from the French *discours* and used by some recent critics for 'writing' considered as a system of communication, as used in the statement: 'Poetic *discourse* differs from other types of *discourse*.' See *semiotics* and *structuralism*

dissociation of sensibility: T. S. Eliot maintained that the power to unite thoughts and feelings had been lost to poets after the seventeenth century

drama: any kind of work designed to be performed on stage, though usually of a serious nature

dramatic monologue: a poem in which a single speaker (who is not the poet) reveals his situation and his character; the remarks of other speakers are sometimes implied by what he says. 'My Last Duchess' (1842) by Robert Browning (1812–89) is a good example

elegy: (i) a poem of mourning such as Milton's 'Lycidas' or Shelley's 'Adonais' (both of which adopt the form of Greek *pastoral elegy*); (ii) 'the form of poetry natural to the reflective mind'. 'Elegy in a Country Churchyard' (1750) by Thomas Gray (1716–71) is a meditative, melancholy poem on humble rural life and on the fact of mortality

elision: the omission of a vowel or syllable or the running together of two vowels, for the sake of metre

ellipsis: the omission of words needed to give the full sense. '*In wit* [he was] *a man:* [in] *simplicity* [he was] *a child*' (Pope's epitaph on Gray)

emblem-book: a book of symbolic pictures explained in verses. *Emblems* (1635) by Francis Quarles (1592–1644) combines engravings with religious verses. Emblems were influential in sixteenth- and seventeenth-century poetry where such figures as Love and Death, or the Body and the Soul were presented to readers who knew them from the emblem-books

end-stopped line: a line of verse which ends firmly with a grammatical pause or punctuation mark

enjambement: (*French*) the running-on of the sense from one line of verse to the next

>   I have lived long enough. My way of life
>   Is fall'n into the sear, the yellow leaf
>   (Shakespeare, *Macbeth*)

envoy: see *ballade*

epic: a long narrative poem in a grand style, celebrating heroic achievements. A distinction is made between epics directly inspired by oral tradition such as the *Iliad* and *Odyssey* of Homer and the Old English *Beowulf*, and literary epics such as Virgil's *Aeneid* and Milton's *Paradise Lost* (all discussed above in the sections on 'Literary background'). Certain features were passed on from Homer and Virgil to Milton: the invocation of a muse; formal speeches; catalogues or lists; extended similes which outgrow the point of comparison; the intervention of gods or supernatural figures; beginning the story in the middle (*in medias res*) and covering the early stages later in a narrative given by one of the characters

epigram: a brief, witty, pointed poem, or part of a poem:

> Coffee, which makes the politician wise
> And see through all things with his half-shut eyes
> (Pope, *Rape of the Lock*)

epitaph: a tombstone inscription, or a poem to mark someone's death

epithet: an adjective or descriptive phrase used regularly or emphatically to characterise a person or thing: William the Conqueror; the Blessed Virgin Mary

epopee: *epic*

essay: the term is used for serious extended works and for short prose pieces conversational in manner such as the essays of Addison and Charles Lamb (1775–1834)

euphuism: the features of artificial prose in John Lyly's romance *Euphues* (1578, 1580): excessive use of antithesis, alliteration, and mythical allusion

existentialism: various modern philosophies are covered by this term. According to Jean-Paul Sartre (1905–80) the individual is the true source of values; he must accept the freedom to act for himself – to do otherwise is to act 'in bad faith'

exposition: the opening act of a play

fable: (i) a story, often legendary and supernatural, not founded on fact; (ii) a brief story with a moral; the animal fables attributed to the Greek Aesop (? sixth century BC) have been retold and imitated by many European poets; (iii) certain modern novels with allegorical features have been described as fables

fabliau: a medieval short story in verse dealing humorously with everyday life among common people

fabulators: a term used by some contemporary critics for writers, chiefly novelists, who deliberately draw attention to the conventions they follow in order to emphasise the artificial, illusory nature of their work – its 'fictiveness'

fancy: see *imagination*

fantasy: a work in which the author deliberately disregards what he considers the laws of real life, sometimes setting his story in another world

farce: comedy based on coarse humour and a ludicrously contrived plot, with little regard for real life

feminine ending: an unstressed syllable added to the end of a line of verse, as in 'To be or not to be—that is the ques*tion*' where the eleventh syllable is a feminine ending

feminine rhyme: a rhyme on two or more syllables of which the first is stressed:

> It is the blight man was born for,
> It is Margaret you mourn for.
> (Gerard Manley Hopkins, 1844–89)

fictiveness: see *fabulators*

figurative language: an extension of the meaning of words as in *hyperbole*, *metaphor*, and *simile*

foil: a character who clarifies by contrast the qualities of another

folk-tale, fairy-tale: a story of popular, oral origin often with supernatural features. The Danish writer Hans Christian Andersen (1805–75) was one of several nineteenth-century collectors of folk-tales. Partially successful attempts have been made by analysts of narrative-method to find rules governing folk-tales which can be observed in more literary forms of fiction

foot: a unit of verse in which, in English, there is one stressed syllable, marked /, and one or more unstressed syllables, marked ᴗ. The following names are used:
iamb(us): ᴗ /   trochee: / ᴗ
anapaest: ᴗ ᴗ /   dactyl: / ᴗ ᴗ
spondee: / / (used only for variation)

frame: a structure within which another story or sequence of stories can be told. The pilgrimage to Canterbury gives Chaucer his frame for *The Canterbury Tales*. Marlow sitting with friends in a boat on the Thames gives Joseph Conrad (1857–1924) his frame for *Heart of Darkness* (1902)

free verse: early twentieth-century poets including T. S. Eliot imitated French *vers libres*, writing verse in which cadence replaced strict metre. Lines vary in length and the movement of a verse paragraph counts for more than the rhythm of a line

gallicism:	the use of words or word-order influenced by knowledge of French
genius:	originally a spirit (Lycidas is said to become 'the genius of the shore' in Milton's elegy), it came to mean 'personal leaning', and then 'innate ability'. The present sense of 'wonderful gifts in a rarely talented individual' began among the Romantics
genre:	a literary category or kind
Georgian poetry:	a series of anthologies of verse published in the years following 1912. Rupert Brooke (1887–1915) was the leading Georgian poet. The term is often used to imply feebleness and polite, country interests, but some Georgian poems are good
Gothic novel:	'Gothic' came to mean 'medieval'. The late eighteenth-century and early nineteenth-century Gothic novels of mystery and horror were often set in the Middle Ages
hagiography:	work devoted to describing the lives of saints
Hellenism:	a vogue for Greek culture in the nineteenth century
Hellenistic:	the term is used of Greek culture in the Middle East and the Mediterranean after the time of Alexander the Great
hero/heroine:	the central characters in a literary work – not necessarily good or praiseworthy; the *protagonists*
heroic couplet:	a rhymed pair of lines in iambic pentameters (see *metre*)
heroic drama:	Restoration playwrights influenced by the epic wrote grand and passionate plays which at worst became bombastic. See the section on the Restoration (pp. 45–6)
heroic poetry:	(i) verse in iambic pentameters (see *metre*); (ii) epic
hiatus:	a break between two vowels which can be joined by *elision*
historic present:	the description of past events in the present tense
homily:	a religious address, sermon
Horatian ode:	all stanzas follow the same metrical scheme
hubris:	occurred in Greek tragic heroes who offended against the gods. *Hubris* means pride or overreaching ambition in English tragedy
Hudibrastic:	the manner and metre of the mock-heroic *Hudibras* (1663; 1664; 1678) by Samuel Butler (1612–80); it is a burlesque written in rollicking octosyllabic verse
Humanism:	in the Renaissance, learning – especially classical and philosophical – combined with love of the arts,

	courtly virtue and a tolerance of human nature; today 'humanists' believe that man can only achieve his full dignity when emancipated from religion
humours:	in the Renaissance the particular mixture of four body fluids (blood, phlegm, choler or yellow bile, and melancholy or black bile) was thought to decide an individual's personality and physical type: a man might be sanguine, phlegmatic, choleric or melancholy. Ben Jonson wrote comedies in which characters were so conceived, each ruled by a certain disposition, passion, or eccentricity, decided by the humours at work in him
hyperbole:	deliberate exaggeration, especially in poetry
iamb(us):	see *foot* and *metre*
iambic pentameter:	see *metre*
icon:	an image, often religious
idiom:	an expression or form of words peculiar to one language or period of a language
idyll:	in Greek, a small picture, and so a short picturesque poem often with a pastoral setting. The Sicilian Greek Theocritus wrote such idylls in the third century BC. Tennyson used the term for his series of Arthurian poems *The Idylls of the King*
image:	Latin *imago* means picture. An image is a word-picture or the rendering in words of a sight, sound, taste, touch, or smell
imagery:	the use of images, especially figuratively, in metaphor and simile
imagination:	according to Coleridge, imagination is an organising, unifying principle basic to creativity; fancy, on the other hand, deals merely with arranging the products of imagination
Imagists:	a group of early twentieth-century poets, led by Ezra Pound (1885-1972), who used free verse, were willing to draw their subjects from all areas of life, and aimed at clear precise expression of feelings and ideas in plain language
in medias res:	(*Latin*) beginning a story in the middle. See *epic*
intentional fallacy:	some contemporary critics hold that the life, ideas and intentions of a writer are irrelevant to a proper reading of his work
invention:	see *wit*
invocation:	a conventional appeal for inspiration to a muse or goddess at the start of a poem, especially in epic

irony:	in recognising irony we find a second intended meaning in what is said: it may be the opposite of the literal meaning, or in some way different. A situation is ironic when we sense a difference between appearance and reality, or intention and outcome. In dramatic irony the audience sees a meaning which the speaker does not recognise, as when Duncan says that there is 'no art to find the mind's construction in the face', in the vicinity of Macbeth whom he trusts and who is to murder him
jargon:	technical terms which are unnecessary or over-used
leit-motif:	a recurring theme or image
litotes:	understatement by negating the opposite of what is meant: 'I was not ungrateful'
lyric:	once a song for accompaniment by a lyre. A poem expressing feelings and thoughts
madrigal:	a lovesong of the sixteenth century
malapropism:	absurd misuse of words through confusion. Mrs Malaprop in Sheridan's *The Rivals* (1775) is given to such mistakes, saying, for example, 'as headstrong as an allegory on the banks of the Nile'
masculine rhyme:	rhyme on the stressed final syllables of the lines
masque:	entertainments at courts and in aristocratic houses in the sixteenth and seventeenth centuries in which the courtiers could take part and which involved costume (including masks) and scenery, music and dancing. A short poetic drama, such as Milton's *Comus*, intended for one of these entertainments, is also a masque
measure:	a metrical *foot*, or a metre
meiosis:	deliberate understatement
melodrama:	(i) an operetta; (ii) a crudely sensational play. 'Melodramatic' is often applied to novels
metaphor:	a comparison without 'like' or 'as': 'Iago is a serpent'
metaphysical poetry:	the work of John Donne and others in the early seventeenth century. They made bold use of imagery, often erudite and ingeniously used
metre:	the discipline of rhythm in verse. The commonest English metre is the *iambic pentameter* with five iambs or iambic feet: Sŏ lóng | ăs mén | căn bréathe | ŏr eýes | căn séeː (Shakespeare, Sonnet 18) A trochee or trochaic foot is often substituted for

the first iamb (see *foot*). Metre is discussed in more detail in Parts 3 and 4 (see pp. 86-9, 105-6)

metonymy: the substitution of a word by one of its attributes: 'the crown' for 'the monarchy' or 'the king'

mimesis: from the Greek word for 'imitation'. 'Mimetic' signifies the realistic as opposed to the artificial, or fantastic

miracle or mystery plays: late medieval religious drama. See the section on 'The medieval Church', pp. 35-7

mock-epic or mock-heroic: writing which parodies the style and conventions of epic, applying them to trivial or to everyday events. Pope's *Rape of the Lock* is the best example

mood: the sense we are given of a writer's attitude: angry, melancholy, cheerful. His tone may be different: an angry writer may adopt a cool tone

morality plays: a form of fifteenth-century drama using personifications: Youth, Good Instruction, Vain Delight, Death; the plays often debate an issue between rival values

myth: this term is very freely used by contemporary critics. It has two basic senses: (i) a 'misconception' or 'misrepresentation' which is widely supposed to be true; (ii) a story reminiscent of ancient myth in content or in imaginative force

mythopoeic: the alleged ability of modern writers to create myth is said to be mythopoeic. The term is often used of Charles Dickens (1812-70)

narrative: story; some recent critics maintain that the novel, the romance, the epic, and other narratives have procedures in common which can be analysed independently of their characteristics as genres

naturalism: an extreme development of nineteenth-century *realism*, especially in France and Germany

negative capability: a phrase of Keats's: a writer's ability to suppress his own personality in order to convey natures different from his own

neo-classicism: the term is applied especially to writers of the Restoration and the eighteenth century who admired and based their views on Latin authors, especially on Horace. They were interested in social behaviour, and manners; they favoured satire; they aimed at polite and pleasing instruction in literature as a means to preserve and consolidate civilisation

New Criticism:	in the 1920s and 1930s I. A. Richards (1893–1979) and other critics at Cambridge emphasised the value of 'practical' close criticism of poetry. In teaching they aimed to educate the student's response to particular texts. Literary history was of secondary importance. T. S. Eliot was their chief guide. American New Criticism, based on the Cambridge school, flourished in the 1950s and 1960s
nouveau roman:	(*French*) the 'new novel'. In the 1950s some French writers produced 'novels' without plot or characters, and (deliberately) without clarity. One of their aims was to disconcert the reader by making the familiar seem strange. Alain Robbe-Grillet (*b*.1922) was the most gifted of these 'anti-novelists'
novelette:	(i) a short novel; (ii) a superficial, popular work of fiction
novella:	a tale, longer than a short story, but shorter than a novel
ode:	originally, a poem to be sung; in modern literature, a grand lyric. See *Horatian ode* and *Pindaric ode*
omniscience:	see *point of view*
onomatopoeia:	the attempt in poetry to give a verbal impression of the sound of what is described
ottava rima:	an Italian term for an eight-line stanza rhyming *abababcc*. Byron wrote 'ottava rima' in lines of ten syllables (the Italians used eleven)
oxymoron:	an evocative contradiction-in-terms: 'darkness visible' is Milton's phrase for Hell
palindrome:	a word, phrase or number that is the same when read backwards: 'Able was I ere I saw Elba'
panegyric:	a praise-poem
parable:	a brief story with a clear moral
paradox:	a pointed or witty contradiction in terms: 'The youth of America is their oldest tradition. It has been going on now for three hundred years.' (Oscar Wilde, *A Woman of No Importance*)
parody:	a literary imitation which is designed to ridicule its original
pastiche:	(i) a collage of various passages; also (ii) a work imitating, or parodying, another
pastoral:	a set of conventions in which an idealised countryside provides a calm background for poetry and love, as in the poems of Theocritus, the Sicilian

Greek pastoral poet of the third century BC. Spenser and Milton wrote pastoral poems; Shakespeare's *As You Like It* has a pastoral setting

pastoral elegy: an *elegy* which imitates Theocritus in using pastoral conventions to lament the death of a friend

pathetic fallacy: a nineteenth-century term for the old convention by which nature reflects the mood of human events

pathos: the quality in a literary work which causes the reader to feel sadness, pity or sympathy for the characters in their hardship

periphrasis: *circumlocution*

personification: see *morality plays*. Poets of most periods employ this device. Keats's 'Ode to Autumn' personifies the season in a series of images, beginning 'Close bosom-friend of the maturing sun...' (see p. 85)

Petrarchan sonnet: of the fourteen lines the first eight (the octave) rhyme *abbaabba*; the next six (the sestet), may rhyme *cdecde*. The sestet often answers or develops what is said in the octave

Philippic: a piece of invective, after the speeches delivered by Demosthenes (?385–322BC) in Athens against Philip of Macedon, father of Alexander

Philistine: a term used by Matthew Arnold for uncultured materialists. (The original Philistines are represented as enemies in the Old Testament)

picaresque: fiction dealing with rogues, travellers and adventurers

Pindaric ode: named after the Greek lyric-poet Pindar (*c*.522–442 BC). The length of lines and the arrangement of rhymes are irregular

poetic diction: language used by poets and not in common use. Milton has been attacked for using Latinisms such as 'horrid' for 'bristling' (*horridus* in Latin). In some eighteenth-century poems a girl is 'a nymph', chastity is 'Diana's Law', and fish are 'the finny tribe'. Wordsworth resolved to use plain language. But all poets make more extensive and inventive use of English than is usual in common speech

poetic licence: 'the truest poetry is the most feigning' says Touchstone in Shakespeare's *As You Like It*. Poetry is licensed or privileged to depart from the literal, from grammar, and from logic

point of view: the method by which a narrative is presented. The omniscient narrator knows everything that happens and can reveal the inner lives of all the characters. The first person narrator knows only his own mind and what he sees and hears. A third-person narrator may be restricted in the same way: he may observe the story through the mind of one of the characters. Such restrictions are self-imposed by the author, who is free to 'know' anything he likes

polemic: a contribution to a public debate. Milton's *Areopagitica* argues for freedom from censorship

prosody: the study of verse composition

protagonist: the central character in a literary work; hero or heroine

pun: a play on words (with different meanings) that sound alike: 'They went and told the sexton/And the sexton toll'd the bell' (Thomas Hood, 1794–1845). Puns can be creatively used, as in Shakespeare and in many modern novels

pyrrhic: the name given to a *foot* of two unstressed syllables

quantitative verse: verse which imitates Latin by making rhythm from the length of syllables (in pronunciation) rather than from stress

quatrain: a stanza of four lines

realism: mid-nineteenth-century writers borrowed this term from painting. Realism showed life as it is, however unpleasant; idealists represented life as it should be. The view that real life can be reproduced in writing (taken to an extreme in *naturalism*) has often been challenged

resolution: the part of a play which follows the climax; usually the fourth act of a five-act tragedy

revenge tragedy: a type of Elizabethan drama involving ghosts, madness, and the duty to avenge, as in *Hamlet*

rhetoric: formerly, an art of effective speaking and writing, with carefully studied rules. 'Rhetoric' is still used in this sense in America. Elsewhere it tends to mean 'obvious contrivance' in speech or writing

rhetorical question: the answer is implied by the nature and context of the question: it is a device for affirming a point: 'what wound did ever heal but by degrees?' (Iago)

rhyme-royal: verse with seven ten-syllable lines to a stanza, rhyming *ababbcc*. King James I of Scotland (1394–1437) used it in *The Kingis Quair* ('The King's Book', 1424), a poem influenced by Chaucer who first used the stanza

rhythm: see *metre*. All lively speech is rhythmic, and so is good prose

roman à thèse: (*French*) a novel with a thesis, in which everything is designed to illustrate and support an argument or 'message'

romance: the principal narrative genre of the Middle Ages. In later literature, romance is fiction dealing with characters and adventures which are more glamorous than those of everyday life

romantic: characteristic of romance

Romanticism: English writing between about 1790 and about 1830, although earlier and later writers are often called Romantic. The term is sometimes used as a counterpart to *Classic* in the way that *Dionysian* is opposed to *Apollonian*. See pp. 51–4

saga: a form of prose narrative in medieval Iceland, composed in Old Norse. The term is now used of any heroic story and of any long family history

satire: a work which ridicules vices and follies

scansion: the analysis of *metre* into *feet*. The first line of Byron's 'The Destruction of Sennacherib' is scanned:

The Ăssýr | iăn căme dówn | líke ă wólf | ŏn thĕ fóld

There are four anapaestic feet: the metre is anapaestic tetrameter. In many English poems scansion is more difficult than here. Experts often disagree. Metre is discussed on pp. 86–9, 105–60

semantics: study of the meaning of words and how it can change from one period to another

semiotics, semiology: the study of signs. Semiotics is a recent, interdisciplinary exercise which tries to apply to literature sociological and anthropological observations about how we signal to each other in 'codes' of meaning recognised by a group or class. See *structuralism*

sentimental comedy: moralising plays of the early eighteenth century

sentimentality: in the eighteenth century feelings came to be regarded as a source of moral values and some writers began to make a display of feeling. This cult was developed by the Romantics. The zealous exploitation of pity and affection in Dickens's most sentimental scenes is now widely regarded as tasteless; the term is derogatory in modern usage

Shakespearean sonnet: the fourteen lines are in iambic pentameter; three quatrains are followed by a couplet, with rhyme schemes *ababcdcd efef gg*; or *abba cddc effe gg*
simile: a comparison using 'like' or 'as': 'her words were like music'
soliloquy: in drama a speech by a character alone on the stage or speaking as if to himself
sonnet: see *Petrarchan sonnet* and *Shakespearean sonnet*
Spenserian stanza: the stanza of Edmund Spenser's *The Faerie Queene*; there are eight iambic pentameters followed by an iambic line of six feet; the rhyme-scheme is *abab bcbc c*
spondee: see *foot*
sprung rhythm: a term used by Gerard Manley Hopkins for a metre which disregards the number of unstressed syllables in a line
stanza: verse units of regular length in which the metrical pattern recurs over more than two lines. 'Verse paragraph' is a better term for other sections of a poem. The commonest type of stanza is the *quatrain*. See also *ottava rima*, *rhyme-royal*, and *Spenserian stanza*
stichomythia: the alternation of single lines between speakers in dramatic dialogue; or of alternating half-lines
stream of consciousness: some novelists have represented the flow of thoughts and feelings in their characters – moment by moment – by breaking down the syntax and logical structure of their writing. Dorothy Richardson (1873–1957), James Joyce (1882–1941) and Virginia Woolf (1882–1941) were pioneers of this method
structure: the plan of a work, including plot, design, and everything that contributes to *unity*
structuralism: a term borrowed from linguistics and anthropology. It is sometimes argued that a work is created less by its author than by linguistic and social structures and perhaps by structures of the mind. Some structuralists have tended towards extreme subjectivity, denying that literature has content which relates to the real world and claiming that the meanings of a 'text' are infinite
syllepsis: an incongruous pairing of terms governed by the same word: 'she arrived in tears and a new dress.' Compare and contrast *zeugma*

syllogism: a system for logical deduction. For example: all men are mortal (the major premise); Methuselah is a man (the minor premise); Methuselah is mortal (the conclusion)

symbol: certain phenomena are considered symbolic: lambs, wolves, rivers, storms, journeys. They have always implied more than their literal meanings; a river suggests time; a journey suggests life. A symbol may be created from anything which can be made to stand for some aspect of life

Symbolism: the Symbolist Movement started in France in the mid-nineteenth century and has had a pervasive influence on English literature. The Symbolists used objects to express ideas and emotional states, without making explicit comparisons. A poet would present a scene or an image in such a way that his emotion would touch the reader. 'Transcendental Symbolism' adopted the Platonic concept of a world of ideas beyond the world of the senses, to be conveyed through symbols. Evocation mattered more to the Symbolists than explanation. They hoped that poetry might achieve the abstract quality of music. Many *structuralist* ideas have been developed from Symbolist theory

synecdoche: a part signifies the whole: 'new faces' for 'newcomers'; 'by sail' for 'by ship'

terza rima: used by Dante in the *Divine Comedy*; there are sets of three iambic lines; the rhyme scheme is *aba bcb cdc* and so on. See Shelley's 'Ode to the West Wind' (p. 87)

tetrameter: a line of verse with four *feet*

threnody: a mourning-song

tone: see *mood*

tragedy: in his *Poetics* Aristotle defined tragedy as a drama in which a self-contained, serious action is enacted and which causes in the audience feelings of pity and fear and eventual *catharsis*. The protagonist's downfall is usually brought about by a fault in his otherwise respectable character, or an error of his judgement, which then leads unremittingly to the tragic conclusion. The precise application of the term tragedy is blurred in English literature by developments which have separated it from the Aristotelian tradition

tragi-comedy: a play in which the elements appear to be leading towards a tragic conclusion, but which turns out happily

trimeter: a line of verse with three *feet*

trochee: see *foot*

trope: an extension of a word's meaning as in *metaphor*, *simile*, *hyperbole*, *synecdoche*

unity: a work has unity when all its parts contribute to a single coherent scheme. A complex work may be unified and a simple work which includes irrelevances may lack unity. In the seventeenth and eighteenth centuries critics influenced by Aristotle maintained that a play should respect three dramatic unities: a single action, a single time-span (the duration of the play, or at most twenty-four hours), and a single setting

Utopia: Sir Thomas More described what he thought an ideal society in his *Utopia* of 1516. The word means 'Nowhere'. Samuel Butler (1835–1902) published *Erehwon* in 1872. Several twentieth-century writers have given accounts of 'dark Utopias' in which the worst tendencies of the present are fully developed in societies of the future

verse: (i) a general term for all kinds of poetry; (ii) a single line of a poem. 'Verse' is also used to mean *stanza*, but this usage is not recommended

Wardour Street: a London street where imitation-antique furniture used to be sold. The name is applied to unconvincing versions of the language of the past in historical plays and novels

wit: in the sixteenth century *wit* meant intelligence, the power of invention, and understanding; a *wit* possessed them. The metaphysical poets gave *wit* the sense of ingenuity or fancy. After the Restoration it came to mean 'good judgement'. The modern sense of 'a talent to amuse by skill with words' is narrower than the older usages, for which we have no exact equivalents

zeugma: 'kill the boys and the luggage!' is zeugma. 'Kill' is incorrectly related to the second object. Compare and contrast *syllepsis*

Part 3

Working on set-books

Introduction

Follow three rules: work with a purpose; be selective; and write things down clearly.

After the first reading of a text decide what to look for on rereading. Use simple headings: plot, characters, themes, settings, language; technique, diction, imagery, ideas, mood. Select turning points in the plot, illustrations of character, and quotations which reveal the author's use of language or imagery. (In an examination only a few examples can be given in the time available; look for the best, and for those you are most likely to remember.) Take notes. You can do so copiously at first and pick out the key points later.

Apply the same rules to classes or lectures and to background reading. Read the set-book before classes begin and listen with a purpose. Select from what is said what is relevant to your headings. A good system is to have several notebooks, one for each topic. Keep your notes clear: space them out; make bold headings; reorganise the notes as you progress. Background reading without a purpose can waste time. Ask yourself what you are looking for. Select what is relevant to your novel, play or poems: what you will be able to use. Paraphrase only what fits or extends the work you have done so far. Copy down only brief quotations and only from passages you understand.

Be selective about further reading. Leave critical books to last. In the early stages consult a brief biography or a book on the author's period, rather than a critical study. Time is better spent with a book which seems elementary (but which you understand) than with an imposing work which may be more specialised or more controversial than you realise. *York Notes* provide all the background information and commentary you need at first. Examiners are more impressed by close knowledge of a set-text and grasp of its period than by allusions to critics, however distinguished. 'Writers and their Work'* is a series of essays, available in most libraries, which supply a brief biography and a general account of an author's work. These are well worth consulting. They often contain the best ideas, plainly expressed, from a full-length book by the same writer.

*Published by Longman for the British Council, Harlow, Essex.

Try to make your work for examinations pleasant. Read other books by your set-author. Look at other authors of the same period or genre. If you are studying Keats, read a poem by Shelley. Once away from required texts choose what appeals to you. Make the most of your teacher or lecturer: ask what to read – but also explore for yourself. See a film-version of a novel or play, if you can, but wait until you have read the book because films are often freely adapted. Afterwards think about any changes the film has made and consider what the filming shows you about the book. Go to see as many plays as possible, not only the set-texts. Play-readings among friends can be more valuable than lectures. Professional recordings of plays and of readings from novels and poems are a wise investment. Do not dismiss illustrated books out of hand: illustrated histories and works on an author's world can supply new ideas. Look out for articles on your authors in the better newspapers and weeklies and in the *Times Literary Supplement.* The more enjoyable the activities you connect with work for exams the better. Keep your examination objectives in mind, and select what to jot down in notes.

Make the most of libraries.* Here especially you need to be selective. Read books through at home, although you may have to read some in the library. You should learn how to consult library-books. Go through an index rather than start out from the first page. Find a topic you know already and see how the author treats it. It is good to go into the library with a particular purpose: a problem to solve or an idea to advance. When working effectively you will probably be moving about the reading-room, from the dictionaries to the concordances (specialised dictionaries dealing with one particular author, or group of works), from biographies to histories. A successful morning's work in a library may mean referring to twenty books rather than reading three chapters of one. Get to know the *Oxford English Dictionary* (which you may have to read in the compact version through a magnifying glass). Here you find the changes of meaning words have undergone in the past, with examples of their use, and dates. Try these entries: *furniture, picturesque, sentimental, brave.* Concordances to Shakespeare and to the Bible are reference works to be used often. There are concordances to other authors. If you are struck by the frequent occurrence of a word in your set-book find it in the concordance to see how it is used in other works. This approach can supply clues to a writer's mind.

The following sections supply detailed advice on working with set-books, drama, poetry, and fiction, and on working with background materials. They include advice on what to read and what to look for, and examples of summaries and note-taking.

---

*See George Watson, *The Discipline of English*, Macmillan, London, 1978, where the following points are made at greater length in Chapter 7, pp. 96–105.

Shakespeare

Background

Your edition of the set-play will supply background information. You need to know how to use it. What edition are you to work with? This may be decided for you. Even so you will sometimes want to consult other editions. There are advantages in having a pocket-volume: the Penguin Shakespeare provides a short introduction, commentary and notes. The Arden Shakespeare, published by Methuen, is the best fully annotated series; each volume has an introduction covering textual, historical and critical background, and appendices in which sources are printed. You should examine the information your edition supplies with a view to what you need to know.

You may find a section on Shakespeare's life. Very little is known. Biographers are obliged to speculate, even in brief accounts. Aim to find out what really matters. We know that Shakespeare was an actor-playwright; that he came from a modest provincial home but was on friendly terms with courtiers; that he was practical enough to make money, since he retired to the best house in Stratford for his last years (1611–16). It is possible to find Shakespeare's 'presence' in his plays. He does not use characters to express his own views. But a belief in order and stability, and a fear of social disorder seem to lie behind his work. Consider what happens to Cinna the poet in *Julius Caesar* when the rioting mob mistake him for Cinna the conspirator: 'tear him for his bad verses!' (III.iii.30) someone shouts when he tells them who he is. In many plays civil disturbances lead to the suffering of innocent victims. If Shakespeare feared the fickle and ruthless behaviour of a mob, he clearly respected the dignity of the individual common man and woman. Certainly his heroes are kings and courtiers; but minor parts (the servant who goes to Gloucester's aid in *King Lear*, for example) often show how a servant or a soldier may be nobler than a prince. It is impossible to prove what Shakespeare's religious convictions were; he never treats religious belief scornfully, although extreme Puritanism, like other forms of extremism, clearly irritated him. Shakespeare's 'presence' in his plays reveals a moderate, cautious, but tolerant mind. These points should be kept in view whatever your set-text.

The order in which Shakespeare composed his plays has been the subject of much debate. The list given on the opposite page is that of Sir E. K. Chambers, *William Shakespeare* (Oxford University Press, 1930).

Historical background is a large subject: concentrate on what is relevant to your set-book. Students of *Macbeth* might explore Jacobean views about witchcraft. In this respect the Renaissance was more

approximate date	histories	comedies	tragedies
1590–1	2 Henry VI		
	3 Henry VI		
	1 Henry VI		
1592–3	Richard III	The Comedy of Errors	
			Titus Andronicus
		The Taming of the Shrew	
1594–5		Two Gentlemen of Verona	
		Love's Labour's Lost	
	Richard II		Romeo and Juliet
		A Midsummer Night's Dream	
1596–7	King John		
		The Merchant of Venice	
	1 Henry IV		
1597–8	2 Henry IV		
		Much Ado About Nothing	
1598–1600	Henry V		
			Julius Caesar
		As You Like It	
		Twelfth Night	
			Hamlet
1600–1		The Merry Wives of Windsor	
1602–3			Troilus and Cressida
		All's Well that Ends Well	
1604–5		Measure for Measure	
1605–6			Othello
			King Lear
			Macbeth
1606–7			Antony and Cleopatra
1607–8			Coriolanus
1609			Timon of Athens
			Pericles
1611–12			Cymbeline
		The Winter's Tale	
		The Tempest	
1612–13	Henry VIII		

superstitious than the Middle Ages had been. King James,* who saw *Macbeth*, was especially interested in the subject. Students of the history plays need to know something of the Elizabethan view of earlier reigns. Richard III was probably a decent and competent monarch, but Shakespeare follows the Tudor interpretation of Richard as a monster. There were good reasons for supporting Elizabeth Tudor: her subjects feared political and religious conflict and civil war, and the queen had achieved a peaceful prosperity by means of compromise.

*Elizabeth I reigned from 1558 to 1603; James I from 1603 to 1625. 'Elizabethan' is the term for her reign; 'Jacobean' for his (*Jacobus* is Latin for James). Elizabeth belonged to the Tudor family; James was a Stewart.

Turning to literary background, begin with Shakespeare's sources. For the English history plays he drew on chronicles by Edward Hall (d.1547) and Raphael Holinshed (d.1580). The Roman plays are based on the Greek historian Plutarch (first century AD), read in an English version by Sir Thomas North (c.1535–c.1601). Shakespeare was always willing to adapt his models for greater dramatic effectiveness, but he sometimes followed them closely. Ignorance of sources can lead to blunders. Othello is a Moor in *Othello* because he is a Moor in the original Italian story by G. G. Cinthio (1504–73), not because Shakespeare thought Africans especially liable to jealous rage. There was a ghost in the Hamlet story before it was reworked in *Hamlet*; Shakespeare did not choose to use a ghost. To look at the sources is time well-spent.

The Arden edition of *King Lear*, edited by Kenneth Muir (Methuen, 1972), prints seven extracts from books which influenced the play: a chronicle play, *King Leir*; a passage from Holinshed; several stanzas from *The Faerie Queene*; and other materials. The introduction explains how they have been used. Shakespeare combines two originally separate plots; he condenses, enlarges and reshapes both. A brief survey of sources before reading the play would show that certain underlying implausibilities, especially in the behaviour of the two foolish fathers who know their own children so slightly, come from there. A re-examination of the appendices after the first reading of the play will show how well Shakespeare has made two improbable tales humanly convincing and merged them into a fresh creation. The quality of a Shakespeare play shows up in every parallel with its sources.

Below the text in the Arden edition, and above the editor's commentary, several lines of textual notes appear on each page: for example, 'the fee] Q; thy fee] F' (*King Lear* I.i.161). The first section of the introduction, 'The Text', prepares us for these notes. *King Lear* first appeared in 1608 in a small, quarto volume printed without Shakespeare's authorisation. 'Pirated' quartos of many of the plays were printed during his lifetime. Seven years after his death a large, Folio edition of the plays was brought out, in 1623. But sometimes a quarto gives a better reading than the Folio, and so editing Shakespeare is problematic. The textual footnotes supply both quarto and Folio versions where these differ. (For some plays there is only a Folio text.) Emendations suggested by former editors are given too. There are passages where modern editors still disagree. A beginner need not be concerned with textual details, but he ought to be aware that we have no definitive version of the plays; no original manuscripts have survived.*

The circumstances in which a play was first performed may be relevant to its interpretation. The Arden edition of *Twelfth Night*, edited

*except for *Sir Thomas More* (c.1595), part of which is thought to be by Shakespeare.

by J. M. Lothian and T. W. Craik (1975), gives an account of what is known about early performances. This is a good example of how Shakespearean scholars piece together scraps of historical evidence. The case that the first night of *Twelfth Night* was on 6 January 1601* – the Twelfth Night of Christmas – is rejected by the Arden editors. They quote an entry from the diary of a lawyer who saw the play in February 1601 at a feast in the Middle Temple, one of the legal 'inns of court'. (At this time Oxford and Cambridge catered for boys as young as twelve and students went on from there to the inns.) It is useful to know that *Twelfth Night* was enjoyed by a student-audience who would probably have recognised, as the diary's author did, that the comedy draws on an Italian play† and who would see the title *Twelfth Night: or What You Will* as an offhand allusion to the festive spirit of the feast of Twelfth Night when students sometimes elected a Lord of Misrule; and the students and young lawyers would also catch the play's topical allusions. We can reconstruct the scene at one end of the Middle Temple's hall, beneath a gallery for the musicians who would have been playing before *Twelfth Night* began.

Illustrations are helpful here, and some editions provide plans and pictures of Shakespearean stage conditions.‡ The first commercial theatre in London was built in 1576 to cater for the new English drama in which various styles, Italian, Latin, and English, came together. The public playhouses were crowded, often turbulent places. The raised stage extended into the audience who were closer to the players than in modern theatres. There were no curtains or breaks for changes of scene. An upper gallery could be used if need be; beneath that and behind the stage was the 'tiring house' or dressing room. A different play was performed daily. The players included experienced actors who managed the company and shared the profits, hired men, and boys who took the women's roles. They usually worked with few 'props' (properties) and with no scenery. One reason why the plays are effective on the radio is that the settings are conveyed in the speeches. After watching modern productions we need to remember in studying the texts how different Shakespeare's theatre was.

---

*See L. Hotson, *The First Night of Twelfth Night*, Hart-Davis, London, 1954.
†*Gl'Ingannati* (The Deceived), played at Siena in 1531.
‡See Maurice Hussey, *The World of Shakespeare and his Contemporaries*, Heinemann, London, 1971; and C. Walter Hodges, *Shakespeare's Theatre*, Oxford University Press, London, 1964. Hodges's book, intended for younger readers, has good illustrations based on reconstructions of theatre conditions.

The set-play

Shakespeare wrote for the stage, not for publication and certainly not for the study or the classroom. In reading, keep in mind how it would be on the stage. If you can read in privacy, read aloud and act the roles as well as you can. On first reading go quickly; catch the drift. If you find yourself lost consult a summary,* but not before trying to read the play. The best procedure is to write an outline yourself and then check it. *King Lear* might be reduced to this:

> Lear decides to divide his kingdom among his three daughters, Goneril, Regan and Cordelia, and to spend his old age with each of them in turn, keeping the title of king without the responsibility. When he demands a declaration of love from each of them, Cordelia, his only loving daughter, rebuffs him and is disinherited. She marries the King of France. The Earl of Kent is banished for taking her part, but he returns in disguise to serve Lear. Goneril and Regan prove ungrateful and Lear finds himself homeless and exposed to a storm on the heath. His Fool has taunted him with folly; now his mind fails, but in his madness he begins to know himself better and to learn compassion. Meanwhile Edmund, the Duke of Gloucester's bastard son, has turned his father against the legitimate son Edgar. Disguised as a mad beggar Edgar joins Lear. Goneril and Regan blind Gloucester as a traitorous supporter of the King. Edgar, disguising his voice, dissuades his father from suicide. Cordelia has arrived at Dover with a French army. After a battle Lear and Cordelia, now reconciled, are taken prisoner. Edmund orders their deaths and Cordelia is hanged. Edgar kills Edmund in single combat. Goneril and Regan have become rivals for Edmund. Goneril poisons Regan; then kills herself. Lear and Gloucester die of heart-break.

Having made such a rough sketch of your set-play, consider what is missing. Several points are missing here. Lear and his elder daughters quarrel when they wish to dismiss the King's retinue of a hundred knights. Edgar keeps the blind Gloucester from suicide by persuading him that he has jumped from Dover Cliff and been saved by a miracle. These details might be worked into a revised outline, but a Shakespeare play in summary is almost nothing, as you will see when you reread. The treatment of the story is what counts. Sorting out what happens is the first step.

Do not be put off by hard passages. Shakespeare used simple language often enough to help out the least educated members of his audience; they would have found the richer speeches difficult – as all modern readers do on first encounter – and would have had to guess at

*York Notes provide general and detailed summaries.

many words which were then new borrowings from Latin or French. Key moments are often in plain English. Here are Lear and his youngest daughter:

> CORDELIA: ... Sure I shall never marry like my sisters,
>   To love my father all.
> LEAR: But goes thy heart with this?
> CORDELIA: Ay, my good Lord.
> LEAR: So young, and so untender?
> CORDELIA: So young, my lord, and true.
> LEAR: Let it be so; thy truth then be thy dower [dowry].

For some passages everyone needs footnotes and glossaries. Leave them, so far as possible, for the second reading.

As you reread take notes carefully. Note passages that please or puzzle you. The first might be memorised later: the more you learn by heart the better, and lines which you like are easy to learn. Ask about problems. Take notes on the characters in your play. Follow these headings: motive; temperament; intelligence; awareness of others; self-awareness; change or development; consistency (which is not incompatible with change); contradictions (people do behave in contradictory ways). Then consider how the characters are presented: in what they do; in what is said of them and in what they say of others; and in their language. Speech reveals character. Lear is foolish in his actions but grand in his speech. Language reveals Othello's nobility, Hamlet's morbid brilliance, Antony's generosity, and Orsino's love-sickness (in *Twelfth Night*). Take notes on imagery: the animal images and images of breaking and splitting in *King Lear*, or the images of costume in *Macbeth*. The unity and meaning of the plays arise from the development of metaphors. Key-words should be noted too: 'nothing', 'fool' and 'nature' in *King Lear*. List words which recur conspicuously in your set-play and study the various meanings they are given.

After a second (or better, a third) reading, look again at the sources. Find parallel passages (the Arden Introduction will help). Lear's division of the kingdom in *King Leir* might be compared in detail with Shakespeare's scene. Plutarch's description of Cleopatra on her barge is often set beside Enobarbus's account of her in *Antony and Cleopatra*. Discover what changes Shakespeare has made in the story. Two or three incidents may have been combined; the order of events may have been altered. Ask yourself why. Look again at what you know of the historical background. How could it be used in discussing the play? Consider whether your knowledge of the Shakespearean theatre clarifies your play. The Fool in *King Lear* disappears after Act 3. That would have been necessary if a boy-actor combined his role with that of Cordelia. The use of boy-actors helps to explain Shakespeare's disguisings of girls as pages in *Twelfth Night* and *As You Like It*. If you have studied other Shakespeare plays, consider them. Shakespeare learned from his own earlier work; he often reworked theories, plot-devices and scenes. If you have studied other writers of the same period (or read them for yourself) look for comparisons with these.

Discuss the play with friends. The lightest conversation may produce ideas. Why do Lear's knights fail to help him at Gloucester's castle where he faces his daughters alone? Does Macbeth have a mediocre mind? Is Falstaff (in *Henry IV*, Parts 1 and 2) in love with Prince Hal? Would you rather play Brutus or Cassius in *Julius Caesar*? There is a danger of asking irrelevant questions: how many children had Lady Macbeth? But so long as we remember that they are irrelevant they can be entertaining and stimulating. It is good to exercise your knowledge of the plays in conversation, even if only in game. They are *plays* and were written to be enjoyed. The more you argue among friends the more you will want to be able to quote from memory, and to be accurate.

When, late in your course of study, you come to read critics, look for reliable advice first. Some of the best criticism is plainly written and some of the worst is hard reading. Do not despise a book because it is old-fashioned. A. C. Bradley's *Shakespearean Tragedy*, first published in 1906 but still easily available (Macmillan, 1978), is well worth reading, although Bradley is sometimes old-fashioned. More recent books are recommended in Part 5. Reading other Shakespeare plays, and plays by Marlowe and Jonson, is far more valuable than reading critical books too soon.

It is good to spend some time with a concordance, to explore Shakespeare's use of words in different plays and different contexts. There is more pleasure and profit in this than you may imagine.*

Drama

Background

The best approach to a set-play is to see or read as many other plays as possible. Go to see whatever you can. Read widely and discover what you like. There are some plays every student should read.

Among plays by Shakespeare's contemporaries Marlowe's *Doctor Faustus*, Jonson's *Volpone*, and *The Duchess of Malfi* (1614) and *The White Devil* (1608) by John Webster (?1580–?1625) make good reading. Shakespeare has had no imitators. The best playwrights have admired him and done otherwise. He has had more influence on poetry and the novel than on drama.

*See John Bartlett, *A New and Complete Concordance*, London, 1894; Macmillan, London, 1960.

There are very few successful plays in verse after the seventeenth century. Shelley's *The Cenci* (1819), set in sixteenth-century Rome, and T. S. Eliot's *Murder in the Cathedral* (1935), set in the Canterbury Cathedral of Thomas à Beckett in the twelfth century, are among the exceptions. Most of the best drama since 1700 is prose comedy. Little effective tragedy was written in the eighteenth or nineteenth centuries. In the twentieth century the Americans Eugene O'Neill (1888–1953) and Arthur Miller (b.1915) have revived tragedy. O'Neill's *Mourning Becomes Electra* (1931) adapts Aeschylus's *Oresteia* to nineteenth-century America. Miller's *Death of a Salesman* is a tragedy in ordinary life. Although his *The Crucible* (1953) is concerned with witch-hunting in seventeenth-century America it has been seen as relevant to modern problems.

The wish to make drama relevant and instructive is not new. Ancient Greek plays were both. Commitment is sometimes attacked as a modern malaise. It is said that Richard Steele's sentimental comedy, with socially and morally improving 'sentiments', destroyed the livelier comedy of the Restoration and that a sentimental drama has emerged in modern playwrights with messages. George Bernard Shaw (1856–1950) used the theatre to propagate ideas; his characters spout them. Professional actors complain that Shaw gives them 'too much to say' and that sequences of talk are easily forgotten. Shaw's claim to be Shakespeare's successor was absurd. The excellent *Prefaces* in which he explains his own work show how different he is. At best he has (like many Anglo-Irish playwrights) wit and an instinct for comic situations. One attraction of Shaw is that he can be read fast for pleasure. Begin with *Saint Joan* (1924).

The real objection to plays with messages is that they divide an audience, while the purpose of drama is to unite all present in a shared experience. The best English comedies do not preach at us but exercise our minds and sympathies. Congreve's *The Way of the World*, Sheridan's *The School for Scandal*, Wilde's *Importance of Being Earnest* (1895), and *The Playboy of the Western World* (1907) by J. M. Synge (1871–1909) are plays everyone reads and goes to see when possible.

Sheridan, Wilde and Synge (like Shaw) were Irish, and Congreve was brought up in Ireland. Many of the great playwrights in English are not of English origin. *Juno and the Paycock* (1925) by Sean O'Casey (1884–1964) is an Irish tragi-comedy with an Irish setting. Samuel Beckett (b.1906), whose *Waiting for Godot* (1956) is a modern classic, is an Irishman who lives in Paris and writes in French. *Godot* is the most readily enjoyable of the French-inspired plays of 'the Absurd'. West Africans have recently begun to contribute to drama in English. *The Road* (1966) by Wole Soyinka (b.1934) is a fine play. English talent, especially in the nineteenth century, has been drawn away from the theatre by the rise of the novel. Dickens might in different circumstances have been a great dramatist. His novels adapt naturally for the stage, and for the cinema. Happily there are several lively playwrights now working in London.

The set-play

Read and reread; become familiar with the text. Take notes on period, purpose, plot, characters, themes, and language.

Make a list of period features. Railways were introduced in England in the mid-nineteenth century; motor cars at the beginning of the twentieth. How do your characters travel? Consider attitudes to marriage, and to adultery. Quarrels over women sometimes lead to duels in earlier plays. Duelling was practised in the eighteenth century; by the Victorian period it had almost died out. Consider the formality of relations, especially between the sexes. The Victorians became more distantly formal than their predecessors. English manners have become less formal with every generation since 1900. Ask yourself whether the plot would be possible in another period, and what problems a modern-dress performance might present. 'Props' and social customs may be crucial to the play: these could include swords, visiting cards, or wigs (worn by men in the eighteenth century); chaperons and 'reputation', servants (increasingly rare in England since the 1930s) or social distinctions generally. Remember that a modern audience may be amused or distressed by behaviour which the author took for granted. Look for comparisons with other plays and novels you have read, to build up an idea of the period. Historical films may be helpful (although they cannot always be trusted). Examine histories of painting and illustrated social histories.

A dramatist's purpose may be to satirise, to instruct, to move, to entertain – or a mixture of these. Dramatic satire ranges from the fiercely punitive, in Jonson, to the mildly amused, in Wilde. The satire may be aimed at manners or morals or, in modern drama, at a political system. Didacticism may take the form of polemical speeches delivered by a character who serves as a mouthpiece for the author, as often happens in Shaw. The play may be designed as a whole to teach us a lesson or improve our minds. Dramatists may write from a love of the theatre, from an interest in its techniques, from a wish to renew a tired tradition, or from a pleasure in entertaining. Entertainment as an aim need not mean inferiority – and especially not in drama. Decide for yourself what has first inspired your playwright: an idea or an enthusiasm; a sense of morality or a sense of humour; interest in society or interest in the stage.

Make your own plot-summary. Look for turning points in the action, and for design. *The Importance of Being Earnest* might be summarised as follows:

> Jack loves Algernon's cousin Gwendolen. Algernon falls in love with Jack's ward Cecily. Jack has invented a wicked brother Ernest as a pretext for his trips to London where he is Ernest. Algernon, who has invented an invalid friend called Bunbury as a pretext for leaving London, visits Jack in the country as Ernest. There are two complications: Gwendolen's mother Lady Bracknell forbids her marriage to Jack when she learns that he was found as a baby in a handbag at a railway station. And soon after Algernon's arrival as Ernest, Jack arrives dressed in mourning; he has decided to 'kill' his brother and christen himself Ernest.
>
> When Gwendolen arrives she and Cecily find themselves rivals for Ernest and they quarrel. When they discover that there is no Ernest they unite against the young men. But when they learn that Jack and Algernon are prepared to be christened Ernest they relent. As the couples embrace Lady Bracknell arrives. Algernon tells her that Bunbury has died. Lady Bracknell approves of Algernon's engagement because Cecily is rich. She still rejects Jack who retaliates by forbidding Cecily to marry Algernon. Cecily's governess Miss Prism reveals that it was she who left Jack in the handbag. Jack turns out to be Algernon's elder brother: his real name is Ernest. Jack embraces Gwendolen. Algernon embraces Cecily. Miss Prism and the bachelor clergyman Dr Chasuble (called in to perform the christenings) are also united 'at last!'

This arrangement of the plot brings out the pattern: there are two false Ernests and two girls resolved to love an Ernest. You may find that in your text contrast is an organising principle: *The School for Scandal*, for example, opposes two brothers, the hypocrite Joseph Surface and the good-natured, reckless Charles. Notice how scenes are planned in advance. In the first Act of Wilde's play Jack announces that he means to 'kill off' Ernest if Gwendolen accepts him. That prepares us for the moment (just after Algernon's arrival as Ernest) when Jack appears dressed in deep mourning. Timing is crucial in farcical comedy. Lady Bracknell appears just as the young couples are embracing. Notice how information necessary to the plot is conveyed in dialogue. Sheridan's *The Critic* (1779) includes a parody of how badly this can be done by an unskilled dramatist. In a well composed play the characters outline the situation for the audience in the course of conversation among themselves, but they do not appear to be doing so.

In making notes on the characters distinguish between what we see from their actions and what we hear in their speech. Look for contrasts. Most dramatists use types: the hypocrite, the good-natured spendthrift.

But characters who belong to types can be given individuality. Two or more types can be combined. Lady Bracknell is a draconian snob, a forceful mother, and an illogical-minded woman. These roles can be found in other plays, but Lady Bracknell is an original creation. She is 'static': it is obvious that she could never develop as a character. Like all the cast of this play she has no inner self; Wilde's people are puppets who only remind us of life. Such figures are not inferior to characters presented in depth, and indeed they may be more vivid and memorable. Decide how your author conceived his characters and how well he has succeeded with them. Consider how far the plot relies on accidents and how far it arises from character.

Some plays are more conspicuously thematic than others. Shaw expounds his themes in the *Prefaces*; his characters soon announce them. A theme may concern society or politics (democracy in Shaw's *The Apple Cart*, 1929), social behaviour or manners (malicious gossip in *The School for Scandal*), or a permanent problem of life (divided duty in *Murder in The Cathedral*). In some plays a theme is an argument, as in Shaw; in others it is a meditation – on waiting, for example, in *Waiting for Godot*. Examiners often set questions on themes. Be prepared, with illustrations of how the idea is conveyed in the drama. Beware of thinking about the play as though it were a treatise. Study themes in terms of action, character and language.

Look for varieties of language: standard English and dialect; unobtrusive speech and eccentricities. Most dramatic dialogue is more articulate than ordinary talk, even when the author has made it appear halting or imprecise, uneducated, or just plain speech. Doolittle, in Shaw's *Pygmalion* (1912) complains: 'I'm one of the undeserving poor: that's what I am. Think of what that means to a man. It means that he's up agen middle-class morality all the time.' This is a plain man's speech but we hear Shaw's rhetoric, as well as his views. Comedy relies on verbal wit, epigram and sheer competence. Personal styles of language can be contrasted:

LADY BRACKNELL: ... Is this Miss Prism a female of repellent aspect, remotely connected with education?

DR CHASUBLE: She is the most cultivated of ladies, and the very picture of respectability.

LADY BRACKNELL: It is obviously the same person.

Lady Bracknell sees his chivalrous phrases as a translation of her formula.

Note the language of different characters and scenes. Note peculiarities of language and think about their effect. Watch for features of language which recur: in particular, striking phrases or images, which may also contribute to themes. If you have access to a recording, listen to the cadences of speech, and judge how they reveal the speakers. Mark passages where the wording appeals to you and think about them.

Poetry

Begin with a poem. Wide reading has been recommended for drama; close reading is required for poetry. Scanning volumes of poems has little value at first. Suppose you are to study Keats. If you look at the Odes you will find the 'Ode to Autumn' (1819) the clearest, on first reading:

> Season of mists and mellow fruitfulness,
> Close bosom-friend of the maturing sun;
> Conspiring with him how to load and bless
> With fruit the vines that round the thatch-eaves run;
> To bend with apples the moss'd cottage-trees,
> And fill all fruit with ripeness to the core;
> To swell the gourd, and plump the hazel shells
> With a sweet kernel; to set budding more,
> And still more, later flowers for the bees,
> Until they think warm days will never cease;
> For Summer has o'erbrimm'd their clammy cells.
>
> Who hath not seen thee oft amid thy store?
> Sometimes whoever seeks abroad may find
> Thee sitting careless on a granary floor,
> Thy hair soft-lifted by the winnowing wind;
> Or on a half-reap'd furrow sound asleep,
> Drowsed with the fume of poppies, while thy hook
> Spares the next swath and all its twined flowers;
> And sometimes like a gleaner thou doest keep
> Steady thy laden head across a brook;
> Or by a cyder-press, with patient look,
> Thou watchest the last oozings hours by hours.
>
> Where are the songs of Spring? Ay, where are they?
> Think not of them, thou hast thy music too, –
> While barred clouds bloom the soft-dying day
> And touch the stubble-plains with rosy hue;
> Then in a wailful choir the small gnats mourn
> Among the river-sallows, borne aloft
> Or sinking as the light wind lives or dies;
> And full-grown lambs loud bleat from hilly bourn;
> Hedge-crickets sing; and now with treble soft
> The red-breast whistles from a garden-croft;
> And gathering swallows twitter in the skies.

What can we say about technique? The three stanzas are of eleven lines. Each line has ten syllables. The metre is basically iambic. The endings are masculine – on a strong stress. Each stanza begins like a quatrain with the rhyme scheme *abab*; the remaining seven lines use three rhymes and the pattern varies. Alliteration (on *m* and *s* in the first line) and assonance ('thou' 'oozings' 'hours by hours' at the end of the last stanza) are present but not insistent. End-stopped lines are varied with enjambement:

Who hath not seen thee oft amid thy store?

is end-stopped; but the second line carries over the sentence from the previous line in

Sometimes whoever seeks abroad may find
Thee sitting careless on a granary floor,

In each stanza Keats builds up clauses, broken by semi-colons, in a single extended sentence (except for the rhetorical questions which begin stanzas 2 and 3).

The poem's technical devices are unobtrusive. The rhymes and the regular lines and stanzas seem to fall into place quite naturally. The long, loaded sentences make easy reading: we have a sense of slow, lazy reflection which suits the mood. The long vowels, especially the sounds of 'load', 'core', 'flower', 'brook' and 'fruit', add to the impression of rich fulfilment; but we are not aware of contrivance. The poem is an extended personification of the season, as a maturing force which 'conspires' with the sun to bring about mellow fruitfulness everywhere. Autumn is saluted in return (in stanza 3) by the music of nature. In the second stanza the season is embodied in a series of figures who add to the description of autumnal scenes. Personification is an old device; here it seems new and natural.

Keats is a major Romantic poet; what then is Romantic in this poem? One declared objective of poets of this period was to avoid the artificial poetic diction of the Augustans. The vocabulary here is rich but close to what might have been used in a letter. Keats keeps the old second person singular; word order is occasionally adapted, as in 'treble soft' for 'soft treble'; 'hilly bourn' is 'poetical'; the final -ed is sometimes marked with a light stress ('twined'). But we hardly notice these small freedoms with the living language of the time.

A new approach to nature appears in the Romantics. Although Keats's personification is playful it is imaginative, in Coleridge's sense, rather than fanciful; the poem grows out of the feeling of Autumn as a mature presence. Keats sees the apple-trees bending under the weight of the fruit; he conveys the feel of the wind and the substance of the nuts; he hears the detailed chorus of gnats, lambs and birds. He is not only close to nature as an observer; the maturity and contentment of the season are within him.

If we look at Keats's 'Ode to a Nightingale' (1819) we find the same concentrated sensuousness, but a different mood. The poet envies the nightingale its freedom from human misery:

> The weariness, the fever and the fret
>   Here, where men sit and hear each other groan;
>   Where palsy shakes a few, sad, last gray hairs
>   Where youth grows pale and spectre-thin, and dies;
>   Where but to think is to be full of sorrow
>   And leaden-eyed despairs

Keats had nursed his dying brother the previous year and was himself to die from tuberculosis two years later, at the age of twenty-six. In 'Ode to a Nightingale' he is moved by the bird's song to wish for death:

> Now more than ever seems it rich to die,
>   To cease upon the midnight with no pain,
>   While thou art pouring forth they soul abroad
>   In such an ecstasy!

This was a theme other Romantic poets were to develop; the search for 'rich' experience, in beauty, in nature, in art, in nostalgia, and even in drugs, eventually led to a morbid interest in death. Returning to the 'Ode to Autumn', we notice faint allusions to dying in the last stanza. Autumn is the decline of the year, but here Keats accepts its peaceful, mournful music in place of 'the songs of Spring'. The mountains and lakes of north-west England were for Wordsworth a moral inspiration in later life, though he regretted the loss of an unthinking harmony with them which he had felt in childhood. Keats, likewise, drew strength from nature.

We might go on to look at an autumnal poem by Shelley: the 'Ode to the West Wind', written in the same year as 'To Autumn', 1819. The poem begins:

> O wild West Wind, thou breath of Autumn's being,
> Thou, from whose unseen presence the leaves dead
> Are driven, like ghosts from an enchanter fleeing,
>
> Yellow, and black, and pale, and hectic red
> Pestilence stricken multitudes! O thou,
> Who chariotest to their dark wintry bed
>
> The winged seeds, where they lie cold and low,
> Each like a corpse within its grave, until
> Thine azure sister of the Spring shall blow

> Her clarion o'er the dreaming earth, and fill
> (Driving sweet buds like flocks to feed in air)
> With living hues and odours, plain and hill:
>
> Wild Spirit, which art moving everywhere,
> Destroyer and preserver; hear, o hear!

It has been said that you cannot read Shelley too fast or Keats too slowly. The sentences hurtle through the controlled *terza rima*; this is an example of how disciplined metre and freedom of writing can be combined in poetry. After each set of four units of three lines with linked rhyme there is a couplet invoking the Wind. The energy, speed, and motion of Shelley's autumn show us by contrast how concrete and still Keats's poem makes the season seem. Shelley wants the wind to inspire him with its 'breath' so that he may prophesy to the world. 'If winter comes', the poem ends, 'can Spring be far behind?' Shelley hoped to regenerate society.

The ideals of the French Revolution which had touched Wordsworth affected Shelley far more than Keats. 'I never wrote one single line of poetry with the least shadow of public thought,' Keats claimed, although he also said that he would throw himself into a volcano 'for any public good'. Keats, we need to remember, was a very young man. There is such variety of outlook and ideas among the Romantics that generalisations are dangerous: their opposites tend also to be true. The Romantics were concerned with society, and inclined to escape from it; modern-minded, but in love with the past; intellectual, but nostalgic for childhood; experimental with verse, but also inclined to use traditional forms, such as Shelley's *terza rima*. It is best to concentrate on one poem at a time, remembering that each is unique and that poems are worth more than Movements, however grand.

As you read more of Keats's Odes you will come to see 'Ode to Autumn' in relation to them, and the Odes in relation to the narrative poems. In the Odes he took ideas from his reading and built poems around them: in 'The Eve of Saint Agnes' (1819) he enriched an existing narrative with patterns of sensuous imagery – as Shakespeare had. Go on to look at other Romantic poems: Coleridge's *Kubla Khan* (1797, published 1816); Wordsworth's *Tintern Abbey* (1798); and perhaps an early poem, 'The Lotus-Eaters' (1833), by Tennyson who grew up reading the Romantics. As you make progress you will want to explore anthologies (the Penguin Books of Verse, perhaps). You might specialise in dramatic monologues. In Tennyson's 'Tithonus' (1832) the unhappy immortal laments his condition and (understandably in this context) longs for death. In 'Soliloquy in a Spanish Cloister' (1842) by Robert Browning (1812–89) a monk vents an innocent rage against one of his brothers. T. S. Eliot's 'Love Song of J. Alfred Prufrock' (1917) is a haunting, deliberately bewildering, twentieth-century soliloquy.

Take one poem at a time. Take trouble to examine details of technique: the rhyme scheme, the stanzas, the metre, the diction. We have seen how these contribute to the effect in Keats's 'Ode to Autumn'. Consider whether the rhymes seem strained: an inappropriate word used for the sake of a rhyme is a flaw. In looking at the diction, ask yourself which words, if any, would seem out of place in prose. Why are they used and how successfully? Find words for the mood of the poem, for its ideas, and images. Copy out passages: one observes more in the course of doing so.

Here is an example of how you might set out notes, on the opening lines from Shelley's 'Ode to the West Wind'.

Date: 1819 (Shelley was twenty-seven)
Composed: northern Italy
Stanza: *terza rima*. Units of three lines, linked by rhyme: *aba bcb cdc ded*; a final couplet
Metre: iambic pentameter. Feminine rhyme-endings (with unstressed eleventh syllable) in first and third lines: 'being', 'fleeing'. There is a swift surge in the lines: the reader is carried forward to the climax 'Hear, o hear!'
Enjambement: ... the leaves dead/Are driven ...
   ... O thou,/Who chariotest ...
Personification and imagery: the Wind is personified as 'the breath' of autumn.
The leaves are like ghosts fleeing from 'an enchanter' (sorcerer) and like crowds fleeing from plague. (Excellent)
The wind is a charioteer; a 'Destroyer and preserver'. The Spring wind is the autumnal wind's 'azure sister'. (Conventional, but good here)
Buds are driven on the wind like flocks (of sheep) to 'feed in air': Shelley 'makes the concrete seem abstract'
Hues are 'living'
Diction: The words seem to come naturally. They are carefully chosen although Shelley gives the impression of a spontaneous outpouring of language. Nothing seems artificial, except perhaps 'azure sister'
'Thou' is used, as in all the Romantics
NB 'hectic' (look it up later): feverish
Vocative case: 'O ... wind'. The poem is an address to the wind as a powerful spirit present everywhere in nature
Impression: Incantation; the last words shouted. Swift movement, power and energy in earth and sky. A terrible force (ghosts, plague, Destroyer) which is a Preserver too. Rapidly succeeding images
Idea: Spring is present already: Autumn preserves the seeds which will lie in the earth until spring resurrects them

The novel

Background

You will need some idea of the history of the novel, whatever your author's period. Contemporary novelists are very conscious of their predecessors; the 'modernist' writers of the early twentieth century, who included D. H. Lawrence (1885–1930), aimed to break away from the conventions of Victorian fiction. If you turn to a literary history such as Walter Allen's *The English Novel* (Penguin, 1970) you find that certain concepts recur. Some are social: the growth of a middle class readership; social changes following the expansion of industry and towns. Others are literary: the gradual rise of the novel in relation to other genres. Notes might be made under these headings. They should be made relevant to your set-book or books. A selection of (frequently studied) novels is used in the following notes to show how that can be done.

The growth of a middle-class readership

Increasing prosperity from industry and trade steadily enlarged the English middle class throughout the eighteenth and nineteenth centuries. Middle-class readers of novels included:

1. **Women.** They were not likely to have been classically educated. They wanted to read about courtship and marriage from a woman's point of view. They were interested in the lives of children. They enjoyed romance (of every kind) but also accounts of ordinary domestic routine (visits, tea-parties, managing servants, helping the poor). Many major novelists have been women: Jane Austen, the Brontës, George Eliot (Mary Ann Evans, 1819–80), Virginia Woolf (1882–1941). In *Jane Eyre* (1847) Charlotte Brontë (1816–55) writes of a woman's emotional life and of childhood; romance and 'Gothic' excitement are combined with domesticity.

2. **The leisured.** Novels are time-consuming and they need some degree of privacy. Addison (early in the eighteenth century) called himself a 'spectator' of life. Readers with private means were in that position, with a detached curiosity about the social and private lives of others. The large leisurely scale of the novel favoured the study of psychology – of inner experience.

3. **The moral and the socially concerned.** Middle-class readers of both sexes valued 'respectable' morality, which they thought lacking in the upper and lower classes, and they included many who cared about social reforms, especially in the nineteenth century (this reflects the Puritan tradition). Dickens's *Oliver Twist* (1837) and later novels reward virtue

and promote social reforms affecting the treatment of children and of the poor. *Oliver Twist* showed respectable readers social conditions they might not care to approach too closely themselves.

Remember, however, that novels have always been read by all classes. Dickens's vast readership was only partly middle-class. But the novel was profoundly influenced by middle-class readers and writers.

Social change

The novel is in some respects journalistic. Novelists are as attentive as journalists to new social conditions. Dickens's *Great Expectations* (1860), the story of a blacksmith's boy who becomes a gentleman, is a study of the relations between money and social status at a time of rapid change. Dickens's novels exposed many of the worst consequences of industrial and urban development. D. H. Lawrence in *The Rainbow* (1915) records the changing experiences of an English village with the coming of railways and mines, bringing new opportunities and new problems.

The gradual rise of the novel

As a newcomer, the novel lacked classical precedent. Henry Fielding in *Joseph Andrews* (1742) and *Tom Jones* (1749) tried to find one in the epic.

1. **'Loose baggy monsters'.** The novel has drawn on many genres: on romance, on picaresque adventure stories of rogues, on drama, on the essay, on journalism. *Oliver Twist* has elements of stage-melodrama with a complicated improbable plot, sentimental romance, picaresque adventure, radical journalism, and 'sketches of real life' (like those in Dickens's earlier *Sketches by Boz*, 1836).

2. **'The one bright book of life'.** Later in the nineteenth century Henry James (1843-1916), following French and Russian models, brought artistry to the English novel but narrowed its scope. James's finely designed stories of Americans in Europe and Europeans in America (such as *The Europeans*, 1878) are delicately amusing and intelligently concerned with moral questions among consciously civilised people. James had no doubt about the novel's high status as literature. D. H. Lawrence saw the novel as 'the one bright book of life'. He was suspicious of James's artistry and impatient of Dickens's elaborate plots and happy endings. In *The Rainbow* and in *Women in Love* (1920) he attempted to convey a personal vision of how modern life might be regenerated.

3. **Anti-novels.** After Lawrence's abandonment of the conventional nineteenth-century plot-and-character novel and James Joyce's more

extreme experiments with stream of consciousness (most successfully in *Ulysses*, published in Paris in 1922), it seemed to some critics that the novel was 'dying'. Fiction had only just become fully 'respectable' literature with Henry James, when it was declared disreputably outmoded! A group of 'new novelists' in France in the 1950s attacked plot, character, and the principle of clarity in fiction. None the less, the English novel persists in Britain, America, Africa and other parts of the world as a vigorous, adaptable kind of writing. Gifted novelists have been no more put off by theoretical objections in recent decades than their predecessors were in the eighteenth century. William Golding (*b*.1911) for example, has used a variety of modes and settings. His first (and still his best known) book *Lord of the Flies* (1954) is an adventure story among British schoolboys on a tropical island with moral and philosophical implications. It is widely regarded as 'a modern fable'. Golding and many of the ablest contemporary novelists are conscious of working within what is now an old literary species, but they find ways to renew it, and they still attract readers.

The set-book

Many of the headings for analysing a play can be used for taking notes on a set-novel: characters, themes, plot, language. But consider how a novel differs from a play. What is lost, or altered when a novel is adapted for the stage? Chiefly, the functions of the narrator who presents everything and gives it his 'point of view'. Three types of presentation are considered below.

Great Expectations

The story is told in the first person, by the central character, Pip. In the first chapter we meet two Pips: one is a small boy, an orphan who lives in a blacksmith's forge; the other is a mature, cultivated man, the elder Pip who is remembering and describing his earlier self. As the story progresses the relation between the narrator and the character develops, as follows:

1. Pip's childhood: he is ill-treated by his elder sister, Mrs Joe, and terrorised by an escaped convict for whom he robs the kitchen at home. The narrator treats him with a blend of sympathy and amusement.

2. Pip as a boy: at the house of a deranged lady, Miss Havisham, he becomes infatuated by her ward Estella and begins to feel ashamed of the forge and of the commonness of his friend and protector the blacksmith, Joe. The narrator is sympathetic but self-critical.

3. Pip in adolescence: Pip is dissatisfied with his apprenticeship at the

forge and longs to be a gentleman. The narrator is sharply ironic at the expense of his younger self.

4. An unknown benefactor, whom Pip supposes to be Miss Havisham, provides money for Pip to live as a gentleman in London. He becomes a snob, and neglects Joe and his early home. The narrator's ironic self-criticism helps to retain our sympathy.

5. Pip's benefactor is Magwitch, the escaped prisoner of his childhood. Magwitch has since become rich in Australia, but as a transported man (a convict sent to Australia) he will be hanged if arrested in England. Pip's false sense of social superiority is deflated. As he exerts himself on his convict's behalf, he comes to be less selfish. When Magwitch dies in prison Pip has begun to learn self-knowledge and the gap between character and narrator has narrowed.

6. After years of honest work Pip meets Estella again. Both have suffered and matured. As the novel ends the narrator and the character are one.

We see Pip in depth, as he sees himself. Other characters tend to be, in the distinction made by the novelist E. M. Forster, 'flat' rather than 'round'. They are seen and heard vividly, but from the outside. Many are caricatures. Even those who have some depth and can develop are revealed only as Pip knew them. A different novel might have been written from the point of view of Estella or of Joe. The first-person novel tends to be one-sided.

Daisy Miller

Henry James's short novel of 1879 is a simple example of another technique. Daisy, a beautiful but ill-educated young American lady visiting Europe with her mother, is observed by Winterbourne, a thoughtful, cultured American gentleman who has spent many years in Geneva. But he is not a first-person narrator. James tells the story of how Winterbourne sees Daisy. Winterbourne is observed as well as observing. We judge him by his reflections as we watch him taking part in events and thinking about them. Daisy is spontaneous, charming, and fond of gentlemen; she has no understanding of the strict European conventions by which a young unmarried lady may get to know them. Winterbourne, as his name implies, is cold and careful, and too conscious, perhaps, of European codes of conduct. His reactions, as the narrator records them, heighten the comedy, and the small tragedy when Daisy dies. He has never seen such a girl before. At first he is delighted, though hesitant. When Daisy scandalises the American community in Rome by going about with an Italian who is not quite a gentleman, Winterbourne's sympathy conflicts with his social instincts.

Two sets of values are present in the two characters. James presents both characters with mild satire. His narrative method allows him to balance the European and American values ambiguously. Each is a foil to the other and neither is perfect.

Women in Love

Great Expectations and *Daisy Miller* are both written from limited points of view. Many novelists – including Dickens and James in other books – vary the point of view, moving from one character's mind to another. Others use an omniscient narrator who can observe any scene and tell us the thoughts of any character; he can address the reader, lecture, moralise, or reflect, in his own person. In Fielding's *Tom Jones*, and perhaps in Thackeray's *Vanity Fair* (1848), the omniscient narrators are more interesting than the characters in the stories they tell us. It can be objected that a first person narrator's point of view is not lifelike – James thought it inartistic for longer works – but it can give us a full view of a whole group of characters.

In D. H. Lawrence's *Women in Love* the narrator moves omnisciently among the characters recording their thoughts and feelings in vivid, impressionistic language. He does not intervene to address the reader directly, though we may feel that he uses the hero, Birkin, to do so. But he describes the English midland scenery in his own person and offers analysis of the characters, and information about their backgrounds. Sometimes the narrative point of view is identified with Birkin or with Ursula who loves him, with Ursula's sister Gudrun or with Gerald, whom she loves. Sometimes it moves quickly from one to another of these central figures, or from them to a minor character. In the language and style of the narrative Lawrence attempts to convey the emotional makeup of each of his people. Imagery and reiterated adjectives count for more than analysis. We have the sense of a narrative style rather than of a narrator. Lawrence did not want to adopt a Jamesian, detached point of view; he wanted his vision of life to make an impact on his reader.

Go through your set-novel watching not only characters and scenes, but how they are shown to us. Ask who is addressing us and how the story is known to the story-teller. There may be interruptions: a journal or letters may alter the perspective. A character may take over the narrative for a time while the others listen. Magwitch is given a chapter of *Great Expectations* where he recounts his own life. There may be a mixture of two methods. Jane Austen's *Emma* is partly omniscient and partly restricted to Emma's point of view.

Beginners sometimes confuse the narrator with the novelist, when they are clearly distinct. The narrator may be a villain, or a liar. Some novelists use an untrustworthy narrator in such a way that we can see through him and judge for ourselves. A narrator may be mad, so that we have to reinterpret whatever he tells us. In some books novelist and narrator are closely identified. Even in a first-person novel we may hear the novelist through the narrator. Pip is not Dickens; but his use of English is Dickensian.

Revision

Revision means rereading the books and your notes, and finding new interest in them. One method is to read the part of one character in a play, as though you were to learn it for the stage. With a novel you could read scenes in which a particular character appears. This gives a fresh perspective. Keep your notes at hand, and check them, add to them, or prune them as you read. Pruning notes can be valuable at this stage; in deciding what to cut you think again about the book and about priorities. You might mark pages with coloured inks: essential; useful; marginal.

You will probably reduce lists of quotations too. Too many quotations in examination answers create a bad impression: that you cannot be selective. Brief, apt quotations are best, and should be used sparingly – unless you are to discuss style and language and to analyse what you quote, in which case longer quotations may be needed. Otherwise try to find short excerpts (under twenty words) which have several implications and can be fitted neatly into various contexts. One sentence might serve to illustrate either the author's wit or a character's nature.

Question papers from previous years are understandably fascinating to examinees. Obviously you need to know the format, the rubric and the style in which questions tend to be put. In France a four-hour *sujet* can have a single phrase ('Madness in *Hamlet*') or a single word ('Irony') printed in the centre of the page. In England question-papers are more crowded, with subdivisions and options which it may be well to understand in advance. Previous papers are valuable if you practise with them. It is hard to simulate examination conditions, unless you practise in class, but it is worth trying. Time is vital in a three-hour examination with several answers to be written; you need to learn how to manage the time. However, trying to forecast the questions is rash.

Although examiners in English literature generally disapprove of 'parrot-learning', and although you do not want to give the impression of reciting-by-heart, some points (and quotations) have to be learned. A brief quotation from a critic may be helpful, especially to start an answer. Learn the critic's name, in its correct form, and the title of the book. Then you might begin 'E. M. Forster tells us in *Aspects of the Novel* that . . .' and go on to agree or disagree, or to elaborate. Do not do this too often. Always mark such excerpts with inverted commas and an acknowledgement. (Examiners do *not* expect publishing details, such as 'Methuen, London, 1970'.) Quotations from critics are not *required* and if your memory is already laden with illustrations from the text it is better to do without them. Little credit is given for filling an answer with critics' names; the examiner is more interested in what you say. Headings from your notes, some lists (features of a genre; or of a period), and some critical terms may need to be learned by heart. Mnemonics are handy.

A mnemonic is a memory device: it may be a rhyme, or a code, or a visual image. Awkward spellings can be recalled by an association: 'station*a*ry' means *at a* st*a*ndstill; 'station*e*ry' means *e*nvelop*e*s. Tricks like this can help to recall characters' names (which *must* be spelled correctly) and relationships among characters. In *King Lear* Cornwall is married to Regan; Albany is married to Goneril: remember *CRAG* (from the initial letters of the names) and you will avoid confusing the partners. Mnemonics you invent yourself are the best. It does not matter how absurd they are in themselves, if they work. A more ambitious mnemonic might connect features of Romanticism, using the letters of the word:

> **R**eaction against Augustan culture, verse, diction . . .
> **O**rganic growth of a poem
> **M**iddle Ages: Romantic interest in
> **A**gony: death and suffering in the Romantics
> **N**ature . . .
> **T**echnical experiments with verse forms
> **I**magination . . .
> **C**hildhood . . .
> **I**ndividual, idealism
> **S**upernatural . . .
> **M**en, language of, for poetry. Common men's lives as a subject for poems

This might provide a reassuring start for a candidate whose mind goes blank in an examination-hall.

Other mnemonics depend on visual images. If you confuse 'dactyl' and 'anapaest', remember that *dactyl* is Greek for finger: one long bone and two short: one stressed and two unstressed syllables. (If you know French, *dactylographe* will remind you of the fingers with which the typist types.)

Part 4

Written examinations

THIS PART PROVIDES GUIDANCE on context questions, unseen passages for appreciation, essays on set-books, and general essays. Well-known texts have been chosen. Do not be discouraged if you have not studied the books from which the examples are taken. It is easy to follow the procedure without previous knowledge of the material. Consider how you would treat your own texts, given the same types of question.

Time is a crucial factor in written examinations. You should write practice answers to discover what you will be able to do in the time available. It is usually unwise to steal time for one question at the expense of another. Always leave time for revising afterwards. *At least* ten minutes in each hour should be spent in making notes and planning. Never rush into an answer; those who do rush in usually waste time on irrelevant matters. Look carefully at how questions are worded. Work out just what is expected and how to set about it.

Context questions and passages for appreciation

Context passages must be referred *briefly* to their place in the text. Questions will normally be set on language and style. You will be expected to show how the writer's art and purpose appear in the chosen extract. The first three examples have been chosen because they can be understood out of context; they are related to their settings. The fourth example shows how to deal with a passage when you are not required to have seen it before.

Shakespeare   *Antony and Cleopatra*, I.i.1–17

Alexandria. A room in Cleopatra's palace.
Enter DEMETRIUS *and* PHILO [two Romans who are discussing Antony's reckless love for Cleopatra].

PHILO: Nay, but this dotage of our general's
         O'erflows the measure: those his goodly eyes,
         That o'er the files and musters of the war
         Have glow'd like plated Mars, now bend, now turn
         The office and devotion of their view

Upon a tawny front: his captain's heart,
Which in the scuffles of great fights hath burst
The buckles on his breast, reneges all temper,
And is become the bellows and the fan
To cool a gipsy's lust.

Flourish. Enter ANTONY *and* CLEOPATRA, *attended*

Look where they come:
Take but good note, and you shall see in him
The triple pillar of the world transform'd
Into a strumpet's fool: behold and see.

CLEOPATRA: If it be love indeed, tell me how much.
ANTONY: There's beggary in the love that can be reckon'd.
CLEOPATRA: I'll set a bourn how far to be belov'd.
ANTONY: Then must thou needs find out new heaven, new earth.

1. *'Put the passage into your own words'*
This type of exercise may take two forms: 'paraphrase'; or 'rewrite the speeches in modern English'. If asked to paraphrase, begin: 'Philo says that their general...' If asked to rewrite in modern English, begin: 'PHILO: No, the general's infatuation...' Here we are allowed to choose.
Begin by finding modern equivalents for the old words:

dotage: infatuation
plated: armoured
office: service
front: forehead
reneges: renounces
temper: self restraint
gipsy: whore
triple: third
fool: clown
beggary: meanness
bourn: boundary

You should remember the meanings from your work on the text. But it is possible to interpret from the context. **Dotage** is not likely to mean senility here; Antony is not Lear. ('To dote on' still means 'to adore'.) Why would Mars 'glow'? His armour would shine. **Office** cannot mean place of work here. There are three 'triumvirs' or joint rulers of the Roman empire in the play and Antony is one of them: **triple** must here mean 'one in three', not 'three-fold'. There are professional **fools**, or jesters, in several of Shakespeare's plays; 'clown' in contemporary English is not an exact equivalent – 'hired comedian' might be better. You must show that the meaning here is not 'idiot'. You might retain

gipsy. You might guess that **beggary** here means 'niggardliness'.
Next summarise what is said:

> Philo thinks that Antony's excessive infatuation with Cleopatra has reduced a great general and world ruler to the level of a whore's hired comedian. Cleopatra enters asking Antony how much he loves her. Calculation in love suggests meanness, he tells her. There are no limits to his love, in this world.

Now you can write a full version. A paraphrase is easier:

> Philo says that the general's infatuation has gone too far. His great eyes, which once shone as brightly as Mars in armour over the troops lined up in battle, are now reduced to gazing – dutifully – on a dusky face. He has renounced all control of his captain's spirit, which used to burst the buckles off his breastplate when he was fighting in battle, and set it to cooling [blowing and fanning cool] the lust of a gipsy-girl. Philo asks Demetrius just to look at the new Antony (now approaching): a joint-ruler of the empire has been turned into a strumpet's hired comedian.
>
> As Cleopatra enters she asks Antony how much he loves her. Estimating love is for niggards, he says. She wants to know what limits he will go to in his love. She will not find them in this world, he tells her.

Now check the details and consider changes. The role of the Roman god Mars is well known, but you might write 'god of war' to show that you know. 'Face' will serve for 'forehead' because he cannot gaze on one and not on the other. 'Brow' is more exact and examiners want exactness. Substitute 'brow'. 'Spirit' has the sense of courage and manliness in *heart* and fits the image of the bellows and fan. That will do. A bellows was used to cool (though later to kindle). We want to make it clear that we know this: 'cooling bellows' might be introduced, perhaps. You may need to write out a fresh version; the first should be done quickly enough to permit that if necessary. If you write your first draft boldly and well spaced out, you can then add a few corrections legibly, and so save time.

A rendering in direct speech in contemporary English is more difficult. The problem is to make the speakers sound natural. What would Philo say for 'goodly eyes'? We might try: 'think of those eyes of his! Shining over the ranks of the field . . .' But we must not be too free. It is better to show understanding of the text than to produce something an actor might convincingly say. Recast the paraphrase in direct speech for yourself.

2. *What is Philo's attitude to Antony?*
List the points to be made. Philo admires Antony as a great soldier, a

man of courage, spirit and strength; and as a leader. He respects Antony's position as a joint-ruler of the empire. He is enthusiastic about the old Antony; he speaks warmly, with love. There is an awe at his general's power: 'the triple pillar of the world'. He would disapprove – it seems – of any such infatuation over a foreign strumpet, especially in a Roman officer who should be able to discipline himself. But for a general and such a general as this, a godlike man, to descend to the level of a common comedian in a prostitute's pay, is terrible, and Philo is deeply disturbed. Antony is wronging himself, and Philo feels wronged too.

His tone should be indicated. The first clause should be said with hot indignation. The memories of battle are said with relish. The references to Cleopatra are angry and contemptuous. He repeats 'Look... behold... see' as though Antony's behaviour is scarcely credible. Now write out your paragraphs, stressing the mixture of emotions: love of Antony and horror at what he has become. Finish by saying that Philo is used here as a typical Roman and as a typical friend of Antony.

3. *Consider this passage in its context*
The opening lines are easily placed. But knowledge of the play is being tested. Later in the first scene we learn that Demetrius has arrived from Rome where people are speaking badly of Antony, as we shall see in Caesar's speech at the start of Act I, Scene iv. We should explain that this scene continues with a dialogue between Antony and Cleopatra in which she cleverly manoeuvres him into ignoring messengers from Rome; while Philo and Demetrius look on he expresses his passion for her and his confidence that (as he kisses her) 'the nobleness of life is to do thus', and that 'kingdoms are clay'. It concludes with Demetrius hoping for better conduct from Antony tomorrow.

That is relevant because Philo's speech and the lovers' opening words are a preparation for the first scene and for the whole play. Shakespeare often begins with two minor characters in mid-conversation to set the scene for the entry of the major figures; Philo interprets Antony from outside: he is disgracing himself. When Antony enters with Cleopatra we hear his grand indifference to Philo's standards. His hyperbole is real to him. 'Bourns', or frontiers, are trivial things to Antony who rules a third of the world; it seems poor-spirited to set limits to love because he is used to sweeping over them in his conquests. It is sometimes argued that the play is not about love but about success. In this opening passage we have the plain man's view that Antony has failed to live up to his reputation and we hear Antony's intention to succeed as a lover as magnificently as in the wars. He does nothing meanly; the generosity we see later when he returns Enobarbus's treasure can be heard in his first line. The opening leaves us wondering: are we to accept Philo's verdict, or to admire the nobleness of Antony's love? Cleopatra's flirtatiousness – '*how much* do you love me?' – can be heard at once. She is a courtesan, as the play will show, but she is also a queen and she speaks as though negotiating territory. The worst that can be said of her has been said already; we watch to see why Antony loves her.

To put the passage in its context you need to relate it to the scene as a whole (our first view of the lovers) and to the play. Rome and Egypt are not only settings but themes and rich sources of metaphor. Here we have a Roman in Egypt giving a Roman view of his leader's debasement before his 'Egypt' (as Antony calls Cleopatra). Rome is to represent reason, moderation, discipline, and power through warrior virtues; Cleopatra's Alexandria is to represent extravagance, spontaneity, and passion. We have both symbols in the lines of Philo and Antony.

Keep reading the passage; as you do so new points will occur to you.

4. *Comment on the language and style*

Look at the vocabulary, and at the syntax. Remember the difficulties of paraphrasing. There is no modern equivalent for **goodly**: 'splendid', 'fine', 'noble' are feeble, especially for a man's eyes. **Mars** seems natural in Shakespeare's English as well as in the Roman Philo's speech, but would be artificial today. **Scuffles** is a good word in the context, apparently stronger when Shakespeare used it than it is now, with its hint of schoolboys outside a classroom. English in 1607 still distinguished between Philo's polite, formal **you** and the intimate **thou** of the lovers (as French does with *vous* and *tu* today). **Bourn** has already been noticed as an appropriate word. Observe the antithesis in Philo's first sentence, and the rhetorical structure which opposes Antony's past and present.

Comment on the verse. Philo talks forcefully, with natural speech-rhythms which fit the blank verse. His sentences are run over the line-endings; the first endstop is in his tenth line. 'To cool a gipsy's lust' parallels 'Upon a tawny front', with an exasperated break in the metre each time as he thinks of Cleopatra. Antony and Cleopatra alternate lines. This stichomythia, contrasted to the enjambement of Philo's brisk speech, suits their private love-talk.

Shakespeare's characters express themselves in metaphor and their images contribute to the poetic structure of the plays. Philo's first figure of speech, 'o'erflows the measure', suggests wasteful excess: the wine Antony spills in his revels, and also the abundance of the Nile, referred to in later passages. 'Mars' is the first of many references to the gods which imply that Antony is godlike ('His rear'd arm/Crested the world' Cleopatra declares after his death). 'Pillar of the world' might remind us of Atlas and Hercules. Even armour is not strong enough to hold together when Antony is fighting in it. Shakespeare means us to accept

Antony as an heroic figure whose fall will disturb the empire. The imagery of the opening passages begins to create that impression. 'New heaven, new earth', he says, and he will soon be speaking of letting Rome melt in the Tiber and the arch of the empire fall – so long as he can be in love.

Modern drama   Oscar Wilde, *The Importance of Being Earnest*, Act I

A brief account of the play is given in the section on 'Drama' in Part 3. In this scene Lady Bracknell interviews Jack who wishes to marry her daughter. So far Jack has satisfied all Lady Bracknell's requirements: he is rich, leisured, and without opinions.

LADY BRACKNELL: . . . Now to minor matters. Are your parents living?

JACK: I have lost both my parents.

LADY BRACKNELL: To lose one parent, Mr Worthing, may be regarded as a misfortune; to lose both looks like carelessness. Who was your father? He was evidently a man of some wealth. Was he born in what the Radical papers call the purple of commerce, or did he rise from the ranks of the aristocracy?

JACK: I am afraid I really don't know. The fact is, Lady Bracknell, I said I had lost my parents. It would be nearer the truth to say that my parents seem to have lost me . . . I don't actually know who I am by birth. I was . . . well, I was found.

LADY BRACKNELL: Found!

JACK: The late Mr Thomas Cardew, an old gentleman of a very charitable and kindly disposition, found me, and gave me the name of Worthing, because he happened to have a first-class ticket for Worthing in his pocket at the time. Worthing is a place in Sussex. It is a seaside resort.

LADY BRACKNELL: Where did the charitable gentleman who had a first-class ticket for this seaside resort find you?

JACK [*gravely*]: In a hand-bag.

LADY BRACKNELL: A hand-bag?

JACK [*very seriously*]: Yes, Lady Bracknell. I was in a hand-bag – a somewhat large, black leather hand-bag, with handles to it – an ordinary hand-bag, in fact.

LADY BRACKNELL: In what locality did this Mr James, or Thomas, Cardew come across this ordinary hand-bag?

JACK: In the cloak-room at Victoria Station. It was given to him in mistake for his own.

LADY BRACKNELL: The cloak-room at Victoria Station?

JACK: Yes. The Brighton line.

LADY BRACKNELL: The line is immaterial. Mr Worthing I confess I feel somewhat bewildered by what you have just told me. To be born, or at any rate, bred in a hand-bag, whether it had handles or not, seems to me to display a contempt for the ordinary decencies of family life that reminds one of the worst excesses of the French Revolution. And I presume you know what that unfortunate movement led to? As for the particular locality in which the hand-bag was found, a cloak-room at a railway station might serve to conceal a social indiscretion – has probably, indeed, been used for that purpose before now – but it could hardly be regarded as an assured basis for a recognized position in good society.

JACK: May I ask you then what you would advise me to do? I need hardly say I would do anything in the world to ensure Gwendolen's happiness.

LADY BRACKNELL: I would strongly advise you, Mr Worthing, to try and acquire some relations as soon as possible, and to make a definite effort to produce at any rate one parent, of either sex, before the season is quite over.

JACK: Well, I don't see how I could possibly manage to do that. I can produce the hand-bag at any moment. It is in my dressing room at home. I really think that should satisfy you, Lady Bracknell.

LADY BRACKNELL: Me, sir! What has it to do with me? You can hardly imagine that I and Lord Bracknell would dream of allowing our only daughter – a girl brought up with the utmost care – to marry into a cloak-room, and form an alliance with a parcel? Good morning, Mr Worthing! [*Lady Bracknell sweeps out in majestic indignation.*]

Candidates who have studied the play would be expected to place the extract in its context by explaining *briefly* what has just happened and what follows from Lady Bracknell's displeasure. They might refer to the final scene in which the mystery of Jack's origin is solved and the handbag restored to its owner, Miss Prism, who is glad to have it back: 'it has been a great inconvenience being without it all these years'.

Further questions might concern the characters, comedy, and style.

1. *Show how Wilde's dramatic characterisation contributes to the comedy in this passage*

We could begin with the fact that the characters belong to their period. Lady Bracknell has said that Jack's answers must be all that 'a really affectionate mother requires'. She means that her son-in-law must be rich, conservative and of 'good family'. Here Wilde is satirising the last criterion. A daughter might in upper-class terms 'marry into' commerce, or the army (socially prestigious in Britain), or 'form an alliance' with an old or noble family. But 'to marry into a cloak-room, and form an alliance with a parcel' is, of course, so preposterous that these criteria for suitable marriages are made to look ridiculous.

The satire is gentle. Lady Bracknell is a ludicrous monster and we cannot take her very seriously as a target. She is comic partly because she is given some of Wilde's best witticisms, and partly because she is illogical. Find illustrations. 'Born in the purple of commerce' needs explaining: the audience is accustomed to the phrase 'born in the purple', used of the aristocracy. A man might rise through commerce from 'the ranks' of the middle class. Wilde's transfer of phrases reflects the increasing wealth of big business families and the (relative) impoverishment of the landed aristocracy. Lady Bracknell is comically frank about that. Her illogicality inspires nonsensical epigrams such as 'to lose both parents looks like carelessness'. Her realism (a cloakroom might serve to conceal an indiscretion) blends with her absurdity. She is a caricature, and thus predictable. When Jack admits that he was found, and in a handbag, we can foresee her horror. She is, for the moment, almost speechless. Point out how the comedy builds up as she gradually takes in the story of Jack's adoption. There are several stages. 'Found!' is the first; 'A hand-bag?' is the next; and the climax is reached with 'The line is immaterial!' In performance the actress must be careful not to make the audience laugh too much too soon.

Jack's quiet politeness, and his dignified explanation are a foil to Lady Bracknell's thunderous disapproval. The details he carefully supplies ('Worthing is a place in Sussex. It is a seaside resort') matter to him, even if they are absurdly irrelevant. It is touching that he preserves the handbag in his dressingroom and offers to produce it in lieu of parents. Wilde makes him naive enough not to grasp the nature or extent of Lady Bracknell's objection, which adds to the fun as they talk at cross-purposes. But Jack is well-bred: he is neither angered nor crushed. If he had less poise the delicate comedy would descend into farce.

You could go on to indicate further how the two roles might be played on the stage.

2. *Comment on the style*
Look for lines where the wording has amused you. For instance, Lady Bracknell's reference to the French Revolution is disproportionate. Examine the sentence:

> To be born, or at any rate bred, in a hand-bag, whether it had handles or not, seems to me to display a contempt for the ordinary decencies of family life that reminds one of the worst excesses of the French Revolution.

The form looks reasonable although the content is not. The qualification 'at any rate bred' gives a false appearance of precise thinking, and the sarcastic aside about the handles promises a sensible verdict. The rhythmic clauses seem authoritative. The last words are an anti-climax. The incongruous linking of hand-bag to Revolution is funny because of its absurd logic and because the phrasing is none the less so assured. Nonsense is more amusing when lucidly expressed. Another example of the same technique might be 'form an alliance with a parcel'.

You could also comment on the comic effect of repetitions. 'Handbag' is repeated six times in seven lines. Lady Bracknell echoes Jack's words in her different vocal register, underlining for example the undistinguished social character of 'the cloakroom at Victoria Station' as the place of Jack's origins.

Poetry   Wilfred Owen, 'Anthem for Doomed Youth'

The following sonnet is by Wilfred Owen (1893–1918), a poet who fought and died in the First World War. Candidates who had worked on Owen might be asked to comment on it as an example of Owen's work and as a poem about war.

> What passing-bells for these who die as cattle?
> Only the monstrous anger of the guns.
> Only the stuttering rifles' rapid rattle
> Can patter out their hasty orisons.
> No mockery now for them; no prayers nor bells
> Nor any voice of mourning save the choirs, –
> The shrill, demented choirs of wailing shells;
> And bugles calling for them from sad shires.
>
> What candles may be held to speed them all?
> Not in the hands of boys, but in their eyes
> Shall shine the holy glimmer of goodbyes.
> The pallor of girls' brows shall be their pall;
> Their flowers the tenderness of patient minds,
> And each slow dusk a drawing-down of blinds.

Deal first with technique, because that is easy. The poem is in the form of a Shakespearean sonnet with a variation of the rhyme-scheme in the third quatrain. Like Shakespeare, Owen uses feminine endings to iambic ten-syllable verses – in the first and third lines where the extra syllable is suitably plaintive. Owen has full-rhyme for his sonnet; in other poems (such as 'Strange Meeting') he was a pioneer of half-rhyme or rhyme by assonance. He uses alliteration and echoes (as in pallor and pall) and onomatopeia, strikingly in the repeated use of *r* and *t* in 'stuttering rifles rapid rattle ... patter'.

The octave contrasts harshly with the softness of the sestet in sound and images. Prayer, church-bells, and the choirs of a funeral service are juxtaposed with the sounds of war which drown them. They would be 'a mockery' given the scale and futility of the killing: the first line asserts that strongly. In the sestet the images are of home where girlfriends and families mourn those killed at the front, and (in the last two lines) try to live on with their bereavement.

There is an anger in the opening of the poem which turns to melancholy. Mentioning this would give an opportunity for students of Owen to comment on his friendship with the poet Siegfried Sassoon (1886-1967),* who was angered by the mismanagement of the war into an attempted protest – although he was persuaded back to the fighting. Owen said that the subject of his poems was 'the pity of war'. The poetry, he added, is 'in the pity'. The pity of Owen's short, heroic life is hard to separate from an assessment of his poem. It could only have been written by a soldier.

Some readers find the sestet too soft. Owen was influenced by Keats, and in the flowers, holy-glimmering eyes and pallid brows of the last lines we see something of Keats's less successful imagery. But if the poem peters out at the end, after its bold start, that is not uneffective because Owen means to say that there is no adequate mourning for men killed like animals.

You might want to praise the sestet in stronger terms. If you like it, think out why. Find words for your own reactions. It may be that those who know about Owen's love of Keats are too inclined to attack him as a latter-day Romantic. If you know 'The Soldier' (1914) by Rupert Brooke you could contrast Brooke's sentimental patriotism with Owen's realism and melancholy. Brooke wrote:

> If I should die, think only this of me:
> That there's some corner of a foreign field
> That is forever England...

His sonnet reiterates 'England' and creates rather an unconvincing picture of it. Owen, you could maintain, is writing from a far deeper understanding of his subject, and a deeper feeling for it. If you know the 'War Requiem' (1962) in which Benjamin Britten set Owen's poems hauntingly to music you might discuss that.

Comment – as always – on the language. Comment on the pungency of 'cattle' after 'passing-bells' (bells for the dead). Perhaps there is a hint of 'battle', which would have been too obvious a rhyme. Rhyming 'guns' with 'orisons' (prayers) and 'bells' with 'shells' helps to blend the religious images with images of war. 'Wailing' is appropriate because it is both literal and ironically metaphorical. The eighth line is moving, and 'shires' connects the battlefield with home and so links the regiments, named after counties, and the British counties to which the soldiers will not return.

*Sassoon published Owen's *Collected Poems* (1920) after Owen's death in action.

Fiction   Jane Austen, *Pride and Prejudice*

The next extract, the first chapter of *Pride and Prejudice*, is treated as a passage for appreciation seen for the first time in the examination and not taken from a set-book.

It is a truth universally acknowledged, that a single man in possession of a good fortune must be in want of a wife.

However little known the feelings or views of such a man may be on his first entering a neighbourhood, this truth is so well fixed in the minds of the surrounding families, that he is considered as the rightful property of some one or other of their daughters.

'My dear Mr Bennet,' said his lady to him one day, 'have you heard that Netherfield Park is let at last?'

Mr Bennet replied that he had not.

'But it is', returned she; 'for Mrs Long has just been here, and she told me all about it.'

Mr Bennet made no answer.

'Do not you want to know who has taken it?' cried his wife impatiently.

'You want to tell me, and I have no objection to hearing it.'

This was invitation enough.

'Why, my dear, you must know, Mrs Long says that Netherfield is taken by a young man of large fortune from the north of England; that he came down on Monday in a chaise and four to see the place, and was so much delighted with it that he agreed with Mr Morris immediately; that he is to take possession before Michaelmas, and some of his servants are to be in the house by the end of next week.'

'What is his name?'

'Bingley.'

'Is he married or single?'

'Oh! single, my dear, to be sure! A single man of large fortune; four or five thousand a year. What a fine thing for our girls!'

'How so? how can it affect them?'

'My dear Mr Bennet,' replied his wife, 'how can you be so tiresome! You must know that I am thinking of his marrying one of them.'

'Is that his design in settling here?'

'Design! nonsense, how can you talk so! But it is very likely that he may fall in love with one of them, and therefore you must visit him as soon as he comes.'

'I see no occasion for that. You and the girls may go, or you may send them by themselves, which perhaps will be still better, for as you are as handsome as any of them, Mr Bingley might like you the best of the party.'

'My dear, you flatter me. I certainly have had my share of beauty, but I do not pretend to be any thing extraordinary now. When a woman has five grown daughters, she ought to give over thinking of her own beauty.'

'In such cases, a woman has not often much beauty to think of.'

'But, my dear, you must indeed go and see Mr Bingley when he comes into the neighbourhood.'

'It is more than I engage for, I assure you.'

'But consider your daughters. Only think what an establishment it would be for one of them. Sir William and Lady Lucas are determined to go, merely on that account, for in general you know they visit no new comers. Indeed you must go, for it will be impossible for us to visit him if you do not.'

'You are over scrupulous, surely. I dare say Mr Bingley will be very glad to see you; and I will send a few lines by you to assure him of my hearty consent to his marrying which ever he chuses of the girls; though I must throw in a good word for my little Lizzy.'

'I desire you will do no such thing. Lizzy is not a bit better than the others; and I am sure she is not half so handsome as Jane, nor half so good humoured as Lydia. But you are always giving her the preference.'

'They have none of them much to recommend them,' replied he; 'they are all silly and ignorant, like other girls; but Lizzy has something more of quickness than her sisters.'

'Mr Bennet, how can you abuse your own children in such a way? You take delight in vexing me. You have no compassion on my poor nerves.'

'You mistake me, my dear. I have a high respect for your nerves. They are my old friends. I have heard you mention them with consideration these twenty years at least.'

'Ah! you do not know what I suffer.'

'But I hope you will get over it, and live to see many young men of four thousand a year come into the neighbourhood.'

'It will be no use to us, if twenty such should come, since you will not visit them.'

'Depend upon it, my dear, that when there are twenty, I will visit them all.'

Mr Bennet was so odd a mixture of quick parts, sarcastic humour, reserve, and caprice, that the experience of three and twenty years had been insufficient to make his wife understand his character. Her mind was less difficult to develop. She was a woman of mean understanding, little information, and uncertain temper. When she was discontented, she fancied herself nervous. The business of her life was to get her daughters married; its solace was visiting and news.

1. *Comment on the style of the first two sentences*
The opening sentence is striking; how are we to explain why? It sounds grand, and amusing. Put it simply: everyone knows that a rich young bachelor ought to marry. Jane Austen's sentence is more polysyllabic, abstract, and stately. It resembles a philosophical proposition, until the last words. 'A truth universally acknowledged' seems to need a less homely conclusion. Try another conclusion. If you know Dr Johnson's observation on marriage (in Boswell's *Life*) use that: it is a truth universally acknowledged 'that marriage is the best state for a man in general'. There is no sense of bathos in the new formula. 'Must be in want of' might be followed by 'a noble purpose in life'; 'a wife' comes as a pleasant anti-climax and reminds us that we are about to read the first chapter of a novel, and not a solemn essay.

The second sentence makes the reader look twice at the word 'truth'. From a universal law we are brought down to unmarried daughters and their parents, mindful of the single man's fortune; there is irony in the repetition of this 'truth' because we see their interest. The sentence is phrased so that we begin with the bachelor who perhaps does not acknowledge the 'truth' and finish with the daughters who hope to take advantage of it. The style is deftly amusing.

2. *Explain the following phrases (i) 'quick parts, sarcastic humour, reserve and caprice'; (ii) 'less difficult to develop'; (iii) 'little information'*
(i) *Quick parts* might seem to refer to the qualities which follow, though it does not, as can be seen from the punctuation. You might remember the phrase 'a man of parts' from eighteenth-century fiction and drama. Consider how we use 'quick' of characters: quick wits; quick intelligence. *Parts* means 'talents'. Mr Bennet is intelligent, and tartly witty. The conversation with Mrs Bennet suggests that he is inclined to put a distance between himself and his wife, his daughters, and the rest of the world; hence *reserve*. *Caprice* means that he is whimsical, wayward, and inclined to tease.

(ii) *develop* cannot have its present sense in this context. From the following sentence it is clear that the meaning is 'unfold'. Think of other uses of *develop*: 'develop a film', for example.

(iii) *little information* cannot mean that Mrs Bennet is uninformed about the circles she lives in because her solace is visiting and news. The phrase must signify general information. Mrs Bennet is not well-educated or well-read.

3. *How does Jane Austen present the Bennets?*
We should point out that the narrator is 'omniscient', and prepared to explain the characters although not until we have heard them in

(uninterrupted) conversation. They are dramatised; they reveal themselves in talk. Mrs Bennet has heard all the gossip about the newcomer and is eager to impart it. She is easily flattered by her husband. She is frank about her hopes of a rich son-in-law and barely grasps that she is being teased by Mr Bennet or that he will not share her eagerness to catch the young man. When thwarted she complains of her nerves. Mr Bennet speaks drily ('how can it affect them?'). He enjoys the ease with which he can baffle his wife as he might tease a child. The Bennets are formal, in the manner of their time, but they are used to each other and, although they cannot share their thoughts, they are on polite, friendly terms. Jane Austen's crisp character-sketches at the end of the chapter emphasise the contrast between them. It seems from the conversation that Mr Bennet has developed his mocking, detached manner as a defence and a solace in the course of daily contact with a stupid wife. Notice the strict conventions governing visits and introductions. Mr Bennet pretends not to understand them in order to satirise her blatant designs on Mr Bingley, which he thinks vulgar. The fact that his satire is lost on her does not affect his enjoyment. It helps him to keep his distance.

4. *Discuss the chapter as the opening of a novel*
How should a novel open? The writer ought to attract our interest, establish the tone, introduce the characters, set the scene, prepare for the action, and hint at the themes. Jane Austen does all that.

The writing is elegant and sprightly. The style catches our attention at once. We are ready to be amused. The tone of the introduction is playful and ironic. The last paragraph shows that we are to watch scenes from ordinary life (among the English country gentry) presented by an intelligent narrator who has a sense of humour and also a firm sense of values. Jane Austen's story-teller finds Mrs Bennet funny; she tells us firmly that the woman is a fool. We see too that the novelist has a sense of drama: the scene between the Bennets could be played on the stage as it is written; the narrator adds almost nothing to the dialogue (only one stage-direction). There are two distinct voices and personalities. The Bennets are too polite to wrangle, but they spar in conversation. They are an oddly matched couple. We shall want to see more of them.

We hear of several daughters, and especially of Lizzie, and we may be curious about Mr Bingley's susceptibility. Mrs Long, the Lucases, and the Bennets appear to belong to a country neighbourhood in which Mr Bingley's arrival will cause a small commotion, especially in houses with unmarried daughters. The scene is set for a comedy, but not for a farce. The narrator's prose has an authority which implies that the themes of courtship, marriage, money, and social life will be entertainingly treated from a serious point of view. We shall want to read on.

Essays

Three types of essay are considered here and three questions are used as models. The first is a broad topic and you are supposed to have time to plan in detail. The second, on a single text, is meant to be answered quickly – within an hour. The third is a general question.

There are several rules for examination essays, to be kept firmly in mind from the start.

1. Look carefully at the wording of the question. If there is any ambiguity show clearly in your first paragraph how you understand the question and how you mean to answer it.
2. Write only about the topic. Background details may be introduced in the course of the essay, but they must be brief and apt.
3. Support generalisations with particular examples. Keep a balance between general remarks and illustrations.
4. Be prepared to revise. Always read the essay through to correct slips of the pen, to remove needless repetitions, and to improve on the wording and punctuation. Time spent crossing out unnecessary words and phrases is rarely wasted. Make sure that the gist of your answer is clearly expressed in the first and last paragraphs.
5. Remember that the examiner knows the plot of your novel or play, and that he is probably tired of reading detailed, irrelevant accounts of it by other candidates. Show your knowledge of the work by the care with which you select examples to illustrate your ideas. Mention the turning-points of the story if you have to discuss the plot. Illustrate features of the characters with brief allusions to what happens to them.
6. Use quotations sparingly and aptly.
7. Make a plan before you begin.

Essay topics are sometimes presented in the form of a question: 'Why does Hamlet delay?' That requires an essay in the form of an answer: 'Hamlet delays because...' 'Discuss' is a common instruction. A discussion involves more than one point of view. Your essay should develop different points of view or different aspects of the topic, recognising that opinions vary. You may be asked to 'explain' a problem or to illustrate a theme or technique. The two stages of 'compare and contrast' may be taken in turn or in alternating paragraphs.

Before you begin the essay make notes on the topic and then devise a plan. Rough-paper work is essential. Set down quickly all that occurs to you. Then sort it out into a plan. A second skeleton-plan may be needed for a longer essay.

Major topic

Illustrate and comment on the workings of deception in Shakespeare's major tragedies.

Begin by making notes. List the deceptions you can remember.

Hamlet
1. Claudius has kept his murder of Hamlet's father a secret.
2. Prince Hamlet fears that the ghost which appears in his father's form may be a devil sent to deceive him.
3. He deceives Claudius by pretending to be mad.
4. Claudius plots to have Hamlet killed in England and to poison a sword and chalice for Hamlet's duel with Laertes.

Othello
1. Iago cheats Roderigo, manipulates Cassio, and deceives Othello into thinking that Desdemona is unfaithful with Cassio. He also dupes his wife Emilia.
2. Desdemona has deceived her father in marrying Othello.

King Lear
1. Goneril and Regan flatter Lear into believing that they love him, and share his kingdom as a result.
2. Edmund turns his father Gloucester against his brother Edgar.
3. Kent and Edgar assume disguises.
4. Goneril plots against her husband Albany.
5. Edmund secretly orders the deaths of Lear and Cordelia.

Macbeth
1. As murderers, Macbeth and his wife have to be deceivers.
2. The witches trick Macbeth into a false sense of security.
3. Malcolm tests Macduff's honesty by giving a false account of his own character.

Consider next the question of self-deception:

1. Some interpretations of *Hamlet* represent the prince as a man who fools himself.
2. Othello is blinded by his own jealousy.
3. Lear and Gloucester do not know their children or themselves.
4. Macbeth and Lady Macbeth misunderstand their own characters when they suppose they will be able to live with their guilt.

Now set down your ideas as they occur.

1. Disguise and misunderstanding are also used in comedies. Viola, disguised as a page in *Twelfth Night*, says: 'Disguise I see thou art a wickedness' (II.ii.26–7).*
2. Deception is a widespread literary device. It was present in the stories on which Shakespeare drew.
3. Shakespeare's art was a form of deception. He often compares the world to a stage and reflects on how we act parts in life. Dissemblers in the plays are required to act false roles before the other characters.
4. The devil is the father of lies. 'The devil hath power/T'assume a pleasing shape', says Hamlet (II.ii.594–5). Shakespeare's dissemblers are often said to be devilish.
5. Shakespeare is interested in the human motives of Iago or Edmund. Edmund's bastardy explains but does not excuse him.
6. He is also interested in how characters deceive themselves: Lear, Macbeth.
7. Reality can be painful. Lear cannot bear it. Othello says that he would have been happy if the 'general camp' had 'tasted' Desdemona's 'sweet body' ... 'so I had nothing known' (III.iii.345–7).
8. Insanity can be a refuge from reality, as it is for Lear. Madness also causes false appearances: 'Goneril with a white beard', says Lear (IV.vi.97) when he sees Gloucester.
9. The supernatural produces false appearances: Macbeth's dagger. The witches are deceivers.
10. We all deceive, to some extent. Kent and Edgar deceive to do good. Cordelia's truthfulness is perhaps tactless. Shakespeare knew that a world of perfect frankness would be impossible. Politeness shades into flattery; tact into cunning; ingenuity into fraud. But Shakespeare's best people are naturally frank.
11. Deceiving devices: the handkerchief in Othello.
12. Faces. Duncan: 'there's no art to find the mind's construction in the face' (I.iv.12–13).
13. Language can deceive, in puns and in nuance. 'Glib and oily art' is Cordelia's phrase for Goneril and Regan. Remember Polonius: 'What is the matter, my lord?', asking him what he is reading; Hamlet replies: 'Between who?' (II.ii.194–6). Remember the words of the witches: 'none of woman born shall harm Macbeth'. He believes it. Macduff was 'untimely ripped' from his mother's womb.
14. There is a strong sense of reality at the heart of each tragedy. Characters cannot escape the real world.

*References and some footnotes are provided throughout this section. They are not expected in examination answers.

15. Deception leads to chaos in society and to the breakdown of family relationships.
16. Metaphors, such as blindness in *Lear*, convey the ideas of deception and self-deception.

Make additional notes on relevant background facts:

1. Shakespeare's contemporaries interpreted Machiavelli's *The Prince* as a justification of unethical methods (including deceit) for political ends.
2. Like many of his contemporaries Shakespeare had a strong sense of the value of order: civil war must be avoided. Deception in *King Lear* and *Macbeth* leads to civil war.
3. Catholic priests (especially Jesuits) were suspect in Protestant England because they allegedly prevaricated under questioning. 'One that swears and lies,' Lady Macduff tells her son, 'must be hanged' as a traitor (*Macbeth*, IV.ii.48).

Such reflections should be jotted down (perhaps in your own shorthand) before the essay-plan is drawn up. Other points may occur to you; this is a large topic. These thoughts must now be organised into a scheme. We should keep the plan simple, but flexible enough to allow for discussion. One obvious plan would be to take each play in turn: they might be treated in order of composition (*Hamlet*, *Othello*, *King Lear*, *Macbeth*), but that is not required. The exact dates of composition are not known. *Macbeth*, in its first version, may be the earliest of the major tragedies. You may think deception a more conspicuous theme in *King Lear* than in *Hamlet*. You may want to concentrate on the play you know best, and to treat that first. You might argue that in *King Lear* and *Othello* the main characters are deceived and self-deceiving; that in *Macbeth* and *Hamlet* they are deceivers of others and of themselves. Alternatively you might follow this plan:

1. Deception appears in Shakespeare's handling of plot, character, theme, and language.
2. Plot. Show how the plot of each play arises from dissembling.
3. Character. Lear and Gloucester are credulous. Macbeth tricks himself into the murder of Duncan and his noble nature is corrupted by the fraud. Othello is noble but innocent; jealousy takes possession of him. Hamlet is clever enough to practise ably but so sensitive, morbid, and inclined to introspection, that he finds it hard to act. He bewilders himself.
4. Theme. In *King Lear* deception is involved in the themes of unnatural conduct in the family, of folly, of justice and of painful growth towards self-knowledge. Evil and ambition are based on

deceit in *Macbeth*. Jealousy is a deceiver in *Othello*. Revenge is pursued in *Hamlet* in a court rotten with falsehoods.
5. Language. Lear misinterprets his daughters' speeches. Macbeth is tempted and bemused by the witches' words. Othello is betrayed by the verbal cunning of Iago. Hamlet uses language as a disguise, in which he sometimes loses himself.
6. Deception also occurs in comedy although the confusions are happily resolved. Deceit leads to disorder, and in the tragedies disorder is destructive.

Let us adopt that scheme. Looking back at the preliminary notes, we can improve on it. False appearances can be mentioned under 'the plot'; motives for dissembling under 'character'; theatrical illusion in the 'conclusion'. Here is a revised skeleton-plan:

1. Opening paragraph. Indicates how the essay is organised.
2. A paragraph on deception as an element of plot.
3. Character:
    (i) a paragraph on devilish deceivers and their human motives
    (ii) well-meaning deceivers
    (iii) the self-deceived. Use Lear as the example.
4. Themes:
    (i) a paragraph on *Macbeth*
    (ii) a paragraph on *Othello* and *Hamlet*
    (iii) a paragraph on metaphor.
5. Language: two paragraphs may be needed.
6. Conclusion. Mention comedies and illusory nature of the theatre. In tragedy evil works by deception.

Before starting, list relevant quotations which may otherwise be overlooked in the course of writing.

The first sentence may be a quotation or a pithy summary of what you mean to say. Sometimes a quotation can be adapted. 'Those whom the gods wish to destroy they first make mad' is often applied to tragedy. We might adapt it (and refer to it again at the end).

Illustrate and comment on the workings of deception in Shakespeare's major tragedies.

Those who are to be destroyed, in Shakespearean tragedy, are first deceived. Deception appears in plot and character, in themes and language, throughout these plays.

The plots depend on tricks and deceits. In *King Lear* Edmund is a Machiavellian intriguer who exploits the credulity of his father Gloucester and the honest simplicity of his brother Edgar. Lear is deceived by Goneril and Regan who pretend to love him. The two stories are parallel and interwoven: Edmund's schemes are directed against Gloucester and Lear. The witches plot against Macbeth who plots, with his wife, against Duncan. Macbeth's regime becomes so treacherous that Malcolm is obliged to test Macduff's honesty by pretending to be corrupt: when Macduff shows his disgust, Malcolm accepts that he is not an agent of Macbeth's. In *Hamlet* Claudius conceals the murder of Hamlet's father, and Hamlet conceals his knowledge of it under an 'antic disposition' or show of madness. He uses the players to expose the king's guilt. Claudius plots to send Hamlet to his death in England. When Hamlet outwits him he prepares a fencing-match in which a sword and a poisoned chalice are to ensure Hamlet's death. Iago, a master of 'practices', manoevres Othello into jealousy of his wife Desdemona. He uses stratagems, arranging Cassio's dismissal so that Desdemona will plead for him, and tricks such as the device of the handkerchief – Othello's gift to Desdemona – which Iago plants on Cassio. Iago constructs a web of false appearances.

From these plots Shakespeare creates the characters of deceivers and deceived. The first liar was the devil; devilishness is attributed to Iago and to the unnaturally ruthless children in *King Lear*. Some members of Shakespeare's audience would have considered Lady Macbeth to be 'possessed' by devils in the scene where she invokes 'murd'ring ministers', 'spirits' and 'dark night' (I.v.47) to help her resolve to kill Duncan.* Shakespeare is interested in the psychology of his dissemblers. Iago is a man embittered by lack of promotion and by a sense that he is 'made ugly' by the 'daily beauty' in the life of Cassio who has been advanced above him. He works against Cassio and Othello because he hates others' success, and in his plotting he abuses the talent as a strategist which might have made him a successful soldier. Edmund is another outsider: in the first scene of *King Lear* we hear Gloucester's callousness towards Edmund's illegitimacy: 'I have so often blush'd to acknowledge him that now I am braz'd to it' (I.i.9–11). Edmund's pitiless retaliation has a motive. Lady Macbeth, greeting Duncan on arrival at her castle, is gravely polite – an accomplished and assured lady. In her welcome she shows the self-control and flair for managing men which enable her to bring Macbeth to commit the murder. Like Iago and Edmund she excels at deceit and her gift for it, joined to ambition, is a temptation to her.

Not all deceivers in the plays are villainous. Kent serves Lear in disguise. Edgar tricks his father in the 'Dover Cliff' scene to save him from suicide. Desdemona deceives her father out of love for Othello. Hamlet dissembles in self-defence. The truthfulness of Cordelia appears harsh to many readers and playgoers. It may be justified (and it makes

---

*John Dover Wilson discusses this in the Introduction to his 'New Shakespeare' edition of *Macbeth*, Cambridge University Press, Cambridge, 1947, pp. lvi–lvii.

good theatre) but it is tactless and unlike the gentleness which Cordelia shows later. Some may feel that she might have dissembled a little and spared her father. Shakespeare's characters have to contend with complex problems and simple frankness is sometimes impossible for them. Deception can be constructive. Shakespeare was conscious of the illusory nature of his own art and of how his Globe Theatre resembles life on our globe. Yet honesty appears as a strength in his work. The cutting truthfulness of Lear's Fool is impressive in contrast to the hypocrisy of Goneril and Oswald as they half-disguise their intentions. Frankness is a characteristic of the best people in Shakespeare's tragedies.

The tragic protagonist who is deceived may also be self-deluded, as we see in the case of King Lear. It is only by suffering that Lear comes to know himself. He has a great need to be loved. He regards kingship and fatherhood as privileges which entitle him to be loved. If affection is withheld he refuses to accept reality. When Goneril opposes him he cannot believe that he is in the real world: 'does any here know me? This is not Lear' (I.iv.234). Finding Kent in the stocks he rejects this proof of Regan's opposition, contradicting Kent five times (II.iv.14–25). His mind breaks down when he is forced to recognise the fact of his daughters' ingratitude. Compassion and humility come to Lear in the storm, in the course of his painful adjustment to the real world. In his madness he sees that he has neglected his responsibilities in the past; he pities his Fool and all outcasts; and he broods on the problem of evil. He asks Edgar (as Poor Tom): 'Is there any cause in nature that make these hard hearts?' (III.vi.75). When he is reconciled to Cordelia he begins to learn to love. When she is hanged Lear dies unreconciled to reality but fully conscious of it at last. Regan says of her father at the beginning that 'he hath ever but slenderly known himself' (I.i.294). Lear's character is revealed as he is gradually undeceived about himself.

Deception and self-deception can be seen in the themes of these plays. A major theme in *King Lear* is the sanctity of 'bonds', between father and children and between King and subjects. In violating these bonds Goneril, Regan, Edmund and Cornwall are misguided: the disorder which follows their lawlessness engulfs them. In *Macbeth* the central theme is the power of evil to take possession of a noble man whose ambition blinds him to his own moral nature. The witches deceive Macbeth with an 'honest trifle' into thinking that he will be able to live with the guilt of Duncan's murder. After meeting them he bewitches himself. He has no peace of mind as king because he can no longer bear reality. Lady Macbeth too is naive. 'A little water clears us of this deed' (II.ii.67) she says lightly when Duncan has been killed. 'Will these hands ne'er be clean?' she asks in the sleepwalking scene (V.i.42). Evil in *Macbeth* is a powerfully tempting fraud.

Jealousy in *Othello* is also a monstrous growth which blinds its victim to the real world. When Desdemona protests to Emilia that she has never given Othello cause to be jealous Emilia replies: 'But jealous souls will not be answer'd so;/They are not ever jealous for the cause,/But jealous for they are jealous' (III.iv.159-61). Jealousy is a deceiver. The themes of corruption and doubt in *Hamlet* illustrate the problems which arise from deceit in a different kind of tragedy. The politics of Elsinore are those of conspiracy. All appearances are likely to be false: a curtain conceals a spy; when Claudius appears to be at prayer his thoughts 'remain below'; Hamlet notes that 'one may smile, and smile, and be a villain,/At least I'm sure it may be so in Denmark . . .' (I.v.107-8). *Hamlet* could be discussed as a study in the workings of deceit.

Themes are linked to the recurring metaphors of the poetry. Animal images appear throughout *King Lear*. Goneril and Regan are compared to tigers, to dogs, to wolves. It is implied that their human form is a kind of deception. Images of disease in *Hamlet* suggests that the outer show of normal conduct in Claudius and Gertrude masks their inner corruption. 'Borrowed robes' and related images suggest that Macbeth is a sham king. Othello is black; another kind of blackness is concealed in Iago.

As a punster and as a poet Shakespeare knew that words have double meanings and can be deceptive. Feste says in *Twelfth Night* that a word is like a reversible glove to a true wit. The witches promise that Macbeth will be safe until Birnham Wood comes to Dunsinane and that 'none of woman born' will harm him. Their terms turn out to have been deceptive. Hamlet conceals his thoughts behind wordplay when Polonius questions him. Iago is a master of misleading nuances. He might have seemed Jesuitical to Shakespeare's audience. His speech to Othello about Cassio's conduct in the brawl is ingeniously presented as an attempt to 'mince the matter' of his drinking. He plants suspicion of Desdemona in Othello's mind so subtly that it seems he wishes to hide his own thoughts. He pretends to evade Othello's questions by repeating his words – 'think?', 'Honest?' – so that their implications fascinate his victim. He damns Cassio and betrays Desdemona in Act III, scene 3 with faint praise, and calculated hints.

Duncan reflects before meeting Macbeth, in a famous example of dramatic irony, that 'there's no art/To find the mind's construction in the face' and Lady Macbeth coaches her husband in how to look innocent. Language is perhaps easier to interpret, at least in Shakespeare, since the audience is often meant to catch hidden implications which the characters ignore. Goneril's speech of filial devotion sounds unconvincing to everyone except Lear: 'A love that makes breath poor and speech unable;/Beyond all manner of so much I love you' (I.i.60-1). She speaks, as Cordelia says, with 'glib and oily art' (I.i.224). We see how willing Lear is to be deceived in his gratitude for this shallow rhetoric. Deception here launches plot and themes and reveals character through language.

Disguise and misunderstandings are, of course, present throughout the comedies. Deception is a fact of life in all Shakespeare's plays, as in his sources and in much of the world's literature. 'Disguise I see thou art a wickedness,' says Viola (disguised as a page) in *Twelfth Night* where the confusions are happily resolved. In the tragedies malicious deception leads to evil consequences and to chaos in the family and in society. It is left to the honest men such as Edgar and Malcolm to restore order in the final scene. Deception is disorderly, and that to Shakespeare means that it is destructive.

If you are studying one of these plays – or any play by Shakespeare – plan and write an essay on 'deception' giving a more detailed account based on your set-text.

Minor topic

Compare and contrast the characters of Ralph and Jack in Golding's Lord of the Flies *and comment on their roles in the novel.*

Lord of the Flies, first published in 1954, quickly came to be regarded as a classic. A summary is provided here so that the guidance on preparing and writing a brief examination essay can be followed without a knowledge of the book:

> *Lord of the Flies* is an adventure story and a philosophical novel. A group of English schoolboys, evacuated during a war at some time in the modern era, is abandoned on a tropical island. There are no adults (the eldest boys are about twelve.) They form a democratic community using a conch-shell to regulate order of speaking at their meetings. They elect Ralph leader. Jack leads the former choirboys who hunt wild-pigs. Huts are constructed and a fire on a hill-top is kept alight in the hope of attracting rescuers. A rivalry develops between Ralph and Jack. The younger boys begin to speak of a 'beast' in the darkness. When a dead parachutist is found on the hill his grotesque outline is mistaken for the beast. The group breaks up. Jack becomes the autocratic leader of a 'tribe' who live for hunting rather than rescue. They paint themselves with clay and perform primitive dances. The tribe worship the beast. Jack sets up a pig's head on a spear as an offering. When Simon (a saintly boy) discovers the parachutist and tries to tell the others, the circle of tribal dancers mistake him for the beast and tear him to pieces. Piggy (an awkward, but rational boy) is killed soon afterwards. Jack and the tribe hunt Ralph, intending to put his head on a spear. The island is set on fire

during the hunt; the smoke attracts a British naval vessel which rescues Ralph and the others.

The novel is a mixture of realism and allegory. It can be interpreted as a moral or political or anthropological fable. It takes a sombre view of the strength of irrational fears and aggressive instincts in man.

Supposing that we are to write the answer in an hour, little time is available for preliminary notes. A plan should be devised quickly. With questions in this form, first compare, then contrast, and finally comment. Comparisons and contrasts can be alternated, but that takes more time to plan. Ralph and Jack differ more than they resemble each other. A paragraph will be sufficient for the comparison. The contrast will require several paragraphs. We should plan while making notes.

Comparison: Ralph and Jack are middle-class English schoolboys of about the same age. They are both leaders and at first respect each other. They are both athletic and adventurous. Neither is intellectually-inclined (as Piggy is). Neither is unusually sensitive or meditative (as Simon is). Both are enterprising and persevering.

Contrast: Ralph's temperament is mild; Jack's is fierce. Ralph's background has been secure, relaxed and happy; his thoughts are of home. Jack has been head-chorister in a cathedral choir-school; he is accustomed to discipline; he often seems insecure. Ralph's eyes 'proclaim no devil'; Jack's eyes have 'a mad look' when he is thwarted. Ralph thinks always of rescue; Jack thinks of survival. Ralph wants to be leader to assure rescue; Jack wants leadership for its own sake. Ralph is obsessed with the fire and the conch; Jack with hunting and his mask. Ralph is responsible and kindly; Jack is aggressive. Ralph matures, learning to think; Jack regresses. Ralph has a conscience; Jack has not. Ralph rules by consent and debate; Jack rules autocratically. Ralph's advisers are the gifted Piggy and Simon; Jack's henchman is Roger, a sadistic boy. Ralph is associated with light (fair hair); Jack with shadows and darkness. Ralph is often presented from within; Jack is observed from outside. The reader is likely to share Ralph's point of view.

This might be set down in shorthand (R. fire, conch: J. hunting, mask) and perhaps in two columns, leaving space for afterthoughts. In making any comparison between characters who are strikingly contrasted, also look at how they differ from other people in the book. Cordelia is unlike her sisters, but it is worth remembering that she is also the daughter of a stubborn and difficult father; something of the stubbornness she shows in the first scene appears later in her sisters. Antony and Caesar are both Roman soldiers and men accustomed to power. Point out the contrasts. Consider where the characters differ most: in speech, in temperament; in what they do; in their associates; in images associated with them.

In commenting, bear in mind the literary background. Allegorical works such as *The Faerie Queene* and books dealing with man as a social and political animal, such as Swift's *Gulliver's Travels*, are often mentioned in commentaries on this subject, even though they are very different. Hobbes's *Leviathan* is often seen as a source for the ideas in *Lord of the Flies*. *The Coral Island* (1857) by R. M. Ballantyne (1825–94) gave Golding his first inspiration. He meant to overturn what he saw as the Victorian optimism and imperialistic spirit of that adventure story.

Comment will involve Golding's reasons for contrasting this pair of characters, and therefore some discussion of the nature and purpose of the novel. Ralph and Jack can be seen allegorically: Ralph is a decent, moderate leader who fails; Jack is a ruthless autocrat who succeeds. Allegory is a part of the novel's method. It is also realistic, and that appears in what the boys have in common. Even Ralph feels an urge to hurt and destroy, at moments. Golding's fable depends for its force on our accepting Ralph and Jack as normal schoolboys. We are reminded throughout the novel of the war taking place in the adult world beyond the island; even when they are rescued the boys go back to a civilisation in collapse. That is relevant to Jack's success and Ralph's failure. Remembering the novel's unified, dramatic structure, we can comment on the role of rivalry between Ralph and Jack in shaping the story.

We now have a rudimentary plan but more organisation is wanted. The paragraph of comparison will be straightforward. The contrasts need to be classified, perhaps into five paragraphs.

	Ralph	*Jack*
1.	temperament and background; imagery of light	temperament and background; imagery of shadows
2.	social behaviour	anti-social behaviour
3.	sensible leadership, advisers	ruthless leadership, henchman
4.	rescue; symbols of conch and fire	survival and tribal life; masks
5.	inner presentation	outer presentation

We begin and finish with the point that, although much is made of the contrast, they are convincing portraits of ordinary boys. The paragraphs of comment should also be planned under headings.

1. Allegory: theoretical structure
2. Nature of Man: background
3. Background of war
4. The plot of the novel: it *is* an adventure story

Even if this planning has taken fifteen minutes, the time has not been wasted. More practised examinees will do much of it in their heads, but a paragraph plan remains essential. A note should now be made of quotations.

Compare and contrast the characters of Ralph and Jack in Golding's *Lord of the Flies* and comment on their roles in the novel.

Golding set out to create real boys, not 'cut-out figures'. Ralph and Jack are normal, middle-class English schoolboys of the 1950s. Neither is exceptionally clever (as Piggy is); neither is meditative or saintly (as Simon is). They both like 'fun' and adventure. They are both athletic, enterprising and persevering. Indeed both stick to their preoccupations: Ralph with the fire; and Jack with hunting. They share certain qualities of leadership and are attracted to each other at first, sensing that. Even when they become conscious of rivalry, they feel 'baffled, in love and hate' (Chapter 3). In happier circumstances they might have been friends.

The island brings out the contrast in their temperaments. Ralph's eyes are mild and 'proclaim no devil' (Chapter 1); Jack's eyes assume a fierce, 'mad' look when he is thwarted. Ralph comes from a secure, relaxed home of which he often thinks, remembering the pony and the books in his room. Jack has been head-chorister in a choir-school; he is used to discipline and to giving orders. He often shows signs of insecurity; he sounds like a much younger child when he is in tears, in Chapter 8: 'I'm not going to play any longer. Not with you.' This weakness makes him more aggressive than Ralph. Ralph shares for a moment the wish to hurt when a gang of boys attacks Robert, but he then feels uneasy about it. Ralph has a far more developed conscience than Jack. The contrast is reflected in images: the ugly Jack is associated with images of shadow and darkness; the handsome, fair-haired Ralph is seen sitting in 'scattered light', in a memorable sentence in Chapter 2. Ralph will preserve decent values until the end; Jack will regress.

In the early stages Ralph shows a sense of responsibility for the group, dedicating himself to building huts and preserving order. Jack is concerned with his own success as a hunter. While Ralph is thoughtlessly unkind in revealing Piggy's nickname, Jack is consistently insulting to Piggy whom he despises as a weakling. Ralph instinctively respects the conch as a symbol of order and equality. Jack instinctively dislikes and disregards it.

As a leader Ralph is patient and willing to listen to advice. He learns to listen to Piggy, who can think, and to Simon, although Simon is thought 'barmy'. He matures in his conduct of the meetings, although he does not appreciate the force of the boys' fears about the beast. Jack is an autocratic chief. He beats Wilfred for no apparent reason except to show his power. The 'possibilities of irresponsible authority' excite his henchman, the torturer Roger. Jack's worst characteristics are developed by his chieftainship. But he does understand (and exploit) the boys' fears and need for noisy, violent activities, because he feels afraid too.

Fear is concealed behind the masks and body-patterns of coloured clay with which Jack and his tribe paint themselves. Ralph is bare-faced and independent – though on the run – to the last. There is a symbolic contrast here. The spear in Jack's hand sometimes looks symbolic in contrast to the conch which represents peaceful discussion. Ralph's goal is always rescue and for him the signal fire is an obsession. Jack is concerned with survival but only because hunting is his forte. He wants power, and when he uses fire it is to smoke out the fugitive Ralph in the last chapter.

We often follow Ralph's thoughts whereas Jack is observed from outside. Jack is a more dominant figure especially in the later chapters. The narrative method inclines us to adopt Ralph's point of view. He is the true hero, the first character to appear, and the group's spokesman at the end.

Ralph and Jack are vividly conveyed and while we read the story we share their experiences. But they can be seen allegorically; Ralph is the liberal, democratic spokesman who believes in sense; Jack is the savage-chief, or the fascist leader. As allegorical figures they play parts in the novel as a modern fable in which Piggy represents the man of science and Simon the saint. But *Lord of the Flies* is not such an allegory as *The Fairie Queene*, or the Morality plays, or Bunyan's *Pilgrim's Progress*. A reader might enjoy and admire the novel without considering the allegory. It is an adventure story and a convincing picture of what children are like.

Most readers will see *Lord of the Flies* as a book about the nature of man, a successor to Swift's *Gulliver's Travels* – a sombre fable of the eighteenth century. Some critics consider that Golding's vision of the boys' failure reflects the ideas of Hobbes's *Leviathan* of 1651. Golding has said that he meant to refute the facile Victorian optimism of Ballantyne's *The Coral Island*. He is also contradicting the Romantic concepts of the 'noble savage' and the innocent child in harmony with nature. Jack's success in taking over the leadership does fit Hobbes's theory that man is not social but self-centred and accepts the authority of a 'sovereign' who can protect a community from its anarchic tendencies and from its fears. Ballantyne assumes that his Ralph and Jack will get on with each other. Golding's pair fight as if by instinct. The first picture of Ralph, playing by the seashore and delighting in his island-paradise, seems Wordsworthian. It contrasts with the image of Jack in Chapter 8, painted with clay and brandishing a spear, like a Yahoo in Book 4 of *Gulliver's Travels.**

*Swift's Yahoos are degenerate, mindless men, ruled by rational horse-like creatures called Houyhnhnms.

Throughout *Lord of the Flies* we are reminded of the war in the adult world beyond the island. The boys are rescued by a gun-boat. They will return to a 'civilisation in ruins' (Chapter 4). Golding grimly implies that Jack's aggressiveness, not Ralph's 'decency', has prevailed in the world. 'We're strong – we hunt', proclaims Jack. Even the innocent Ralph in Chapter 1 plays at being a fighter-plane. He is no longer innocent in Chapter 12, but the naval officer appears to be so. The evil which Jack represents is not to be underestimated.

Lord of the Flies is a tightly constructed novel in which events move rapidly, as in a tragedy, towards a conclusion which seems inevitable. The conflict between Ralph and Jack, implicit in their first meeting, comes to dominate the story until Ralph is helpless before Jack's hunters, and Golding's thesis is worked out. The adventure story compels because of this clash of two personalities. Piggy, Simon and the others are always subordinate. Ralph and Jack provide the novel with its basic structure, in plot, and in presenting two versions of man. They stand out from the story in their contrast and we remember, for example, Jack crying in an egotistic rage, and Ralph (on the last page) crying for the death of 'a true wise friend, called Piggy' and 'the loss of innocence, the darkness of man's heart'.

Any of these paragraphs could be cut to save time. If short of time, keep to your plan and try to write something under each heading. The last five minutes must be left free (preferably ten minutes) for checking. The pens of even the best spellers slip under pressure. Names are easily jumbled, producing nonsense. Sentences can be left verbless, and punctuation can be forgotten. Inane wording, such as 'it is important to note that', can slip in (wasting time), and should be struck out when you revise.

General topic

Why do we study poetry?

Such a question tests your knowledge. It cannot be answered except from experience of poetry, or of tragedy, or of the literature of the past. Other general subjects – 'What is literary taste?', 'What is critical objectivity?' – also test what you know, and how well you understand it. Personal opinion counts, as in all literary examinations, but opinion must be supported with evidence. Notice that this form of wording does not ask why *you* study poetry or why we *ought* to study poetry or why we *read* poetry, although it will involve those questions.

It is good to have a store of quotations from poets on poetry (and of novelists on novels and of dramatists on drama). Shelley's *A Defence of Poetry* (1821) includes remarks which have become famous: 'Poetry lifts the veil from the hidden beauty of the world, and makes familiar objects be as if they were not familiar'; 'Poetry is the record of the best and happiest moments of the happiest and best minds'; 'Poets are the unacknowledged legislators of the world.' Shelley's contemporary Keats wrote that 'poetry ... should strike the Reader as a wording of his own highest thoughts' (letter to John Taylor, February 1818). That might remind you of Pope's

> True wit is nature to advantage dress'd,
> What oft was thought but ne'er so well express'd

from his *Essay on Criticism*. Pope's 'wit' might recall Francis Bacon's 'histories make men wise; poets witty', which is from 'Of Studies' (*Essays*, 1597, 1625). There we have Romantic, eighteenth-century, and Renaissance views. T. S. Eliot wrote that '... our concern was speech and speech impelled us/To purify the dialect of the tribe'. Elsewhere he wrote of 'the intolerable wrestle/With words and meanings' ('Little Gidding' and 'East Coker', *Four Quartets*, 1943. One contemporary defence of poetry sees it as the full 'exploitation' of the resources of language. W. B. Yeats's observation that we write poetry when we 'disagree with ourselves' sums up another modern view of poetry.

Some of these claims concern poetry as language and others poetry as vision. Bacon, Pope, and Eliot stress the poet's skill with words. Keats values 'wording', but wording of our 'highest thoughts' – just as Shelley speaks of 'the best and happiest moments'. Yeats too refers to the poet's communication of mixed experience. Shelley calls the poet a 'legislator' because he believes that poetry makes us, in another well-known phrase, 'imagine what we know', and because he agrees with Wordsworth (in the 'Preface' to *Lyrical Ballads*) that poetry is not 'a matter of amusement' as if it were 'a taste for rope-dancing': 'its object is truth'.

These are formulations of why poets wrote, and of why we read them. You may prefer the Augustan emphasis on elegance, the Romantic belief in inspiration, or the modern interest in 'tension' and the 'wrestle with words and meanings' which is nearer to Bacon's concept of 'witty'. You may want to synthesise them, or to devise your own formula, before turning to poems to demonstrate what is meant.

But if these are reasons for reading poetry, we should now remember, they do not necessarily justify 'study', which (in its context) means 'in class' or 'for examinations'. One answer is that study narrows the distance between the reader and the poem. Most poems are removed in time, and in culture, even from English-speakers. Modern poets often expect a familiarity with poetry of the past. Shelley leads us to the 'hidden beauty of the world' but also to libraries and lectures, without which, for example, the modern reader might not guess what Shelley owes to Plato. To enjoy a poem is to want to study its relation to other poems, which may involve other languages. T. S. Eliot and Pope were influenced by poetry in French. Poetry is rarely studied in isolation; students, in English-speaking countries and elsewhere, are learning English, and literature, and history (from which the study of literature is inseparable). Study helps to keep poetry alive and to spread its truths and skills.

Before making a plan, decide what poems to discuss. The more you know by heart the better because you have more freedom to choose. Variety is wanted for a general subject. Everybody knows some lines of Shakespeare. Use what you know. Pope's couplets are easy to remember; his two lines about wit would serve because they illustrate what they say. Any student of poetry should have looked at Milton: he makes a good example because any reader is at once a student. The best passages to learn are those you like and your choice will shape your essay. The following plan uses some of the poets on poetry, a few famous lines of verse, and our thoughts on study.

1. Introduction: Shelley: poets as 'legislators'. A modern defence could be based on 'vision' and language.
2. Bacon: poets make us 'witty'. Study is needed to appreciate how well language is used, especially in older poetry.
   Shakespeare: Othello's courtship of Desdemona
   Milton: Satan on his throne
   Pope: any good couplet
3. Keats: 'highest thoughts' and 'a wording'
   Lines from Shelley's *Adonais*
   Wording and 'vision'
4. Disagreement with oneself
   Lines from Tennyson's *In Memoriam*, and what they teach
5. Conclusion: a modern poet's view of language and feeling – T. S. Eliot. End by saying that we study poetry to see ourselves better and to see language well used.

Shelley's pronouncement from *A Defence of Poetry* makes a good starting-point because it is such a bold claim. A historical sequence from Bacon to Eliot provides a sensible way of organising our 'defence'.

Why do we study poetry?

In *A Defence of Poetry* Shelley proclaimed that poets are 'the unacknowledged legislators of mankind'. They are still unacknowledged – except in schools and universities. English poetry has never been so much studied, annotated, and discussed as in our own time. But a contemporary defence of the study of poetry need not be restrictively academic. It would include Shelley's view that poets enable us to '*imagine* what we know', and to see the world and our hearts afresh. It would also rightly maintain that in poetry language is at its most sprightly and its most resourceful. Anyone concerned with English ought to be interested in that. To pay full attention we must be willing to study.

Francis Bacon writing 'Of Studies' in the *Essays* says that 'histories make men wise; poets witty'. By 'witty' he means 'intelligent' or intelligently aware. Shakespeare's dramatic verse has that effect if we read closely, even in a passage of relatively plain speech, as in Othello's account to the senate of how he courted Desdemona by telling her stories of his adventurous life:

> My story being done
> She gave me for my pains a world of sighs;
> She swore, i' faith, 'twas strange, 'twas passing strange;
> She wish'd she had not heard it, yet she wish'd
> That heaven had made her such a man: she thank'd me,
> And bade me, if I had a friend that lov'd her,
> I should but teach him how to tell my story,
> And that would woo her. Upon this hint I spake;
> She lov'd me for the dangers I had pass'd,
> And I lov'd her that she did pity them.
> This only is the witchcraft I have us'd.

This is so well composed that it looks simple. Almost all the words are monosyllabic. We hear Othello speaking frankly to the senate and Desdemona's 'hinting' words. The rhythms of speech are combined perfectly with the cadences of the run-on lines of blank-verse. The romance, tenderness and shy intimacy of the courtship and the dignity of Othello are unmistakable. There is almost none of Shakespeare's usual metaphor (Othello has been accused of winning Desdemona by 'witchcraft'). His syntax and diction are often much richer than here. The repetitions of 'strange' and 'pitiful' are natural and touching; 'she' and 'I' alternate until joined in the antithesis before the last, confident line in which Othello brushes off the accusation. Desdemona's reported words are coyly halting, though the verse moves on surely. Othello's speech, in the second and last three end-stopped lines is boldly straightforward, as he is. We need to read closely (and to study the whole play) to appreciate how well the art has been concealed.

Milton's 'wit' too informs his art and teaches us to look attentively. Satan enthroned in hell at the start of Book II of *Paradise Lost* is a grand, opulent monarch but Milton suggests that he is an absurd figure:

> High on a throne of royal state which far
> Outshone the wealth of Ormus and of Ind,
> Or where the gorgeous East with richest hand

> Showers on her kings barbaric pearl and gold;
> Satan exalted sat, by merit raised
> To that bad eminence.

The chief of the fallen angels has been raised up, but only in hell. The last two words sum up what Milton intends to show us in poetry. This is an epic and Satan is a major character; he must be grand, yet he is the enemy of God and of mankind and he must not be heroic. The blank verse is stately. The enjambement, with masculine endings to the blank verse, moves us through the sentence with three pauses only in seven lines. The names Ormus and Ind are meant to evoke the wealth and power of Persia and India surpassed by Satan's splendour. The metre of the fourth line stresses the key words: 'Showers on her kings barbaric pearl and gold' – which adds to the effect of the adjectives 'royal', 'gorgeous', 'richest'. Milton is describing Eastern profusion but the impression created is of Satan's 'state'. The sentence is inverted ('High on a throne ... Satan ... sat') and interrupted by the long subordinate clauses so that we reach the subject and verb only in the fifth line. Some readers have found this unnatural to English: an imitation of the Latin of Virgil. But it is effective. 'High' is kept waiting until 'Satan' explains it; we seem to gaze up at the opulent throne, until the blunt, commonplace 'sat' stops us short. It seems an anticlimax after such a preparation. That is what Milton wants. He mocks Satan with the sarcastic 'merit' and the oxymoron 'bad eminence'.

Milton is perhaps the most obvious example of a poet we must study in order to enjoy. Here we ought to know or find out that Ormus was a Persian trading city. Throughout *Paradise Lost* references to classical mythology and to the Bible, and allusions to a wide range of literature and legend require preparation. We learn to negotiate Milton's epic style and to read him closely. One of the pleasures of knowing *Paradise Lost* comes in reading Pope's *The Rape of the Lock* which parodies the style in deft rhyming couplets for comic effect, in telling the story of the theft of a lock of a girl's hair. Pope reflects on his tiny (mock-) epic subject:

> Fair tresses man's imperial race insnare,
> And beauty draws us with a single hair.

Pope's wit is delicate, epigrammatic and elegant: the rhyming 'hair' fits the sense and the couplet neatly. We remember the great subject of the ensnaring of man by Satan (and by Eve); it is a pleasing change of scale. Pleasure in the skilful handling of words is a good reason for studying poetry.

The Romantic poet Keats echoed the Augustan Pope in saying (in a letter of 1818) that 'poetry should strike the reader as a wording of his own highest thoughts'. 'What oft was thought but ne'er so well express'd' was Pope's formula. 'Highest thoughts', the most intense feelings, and clearest perception of beauty were the aims of Keats and of his contemporary Shelley. The Romantics did not want to dress nature to advantage (as Pope says) but to discover and reveal the sublimity of Nature through full exercise of the imagination. Wordsworth reminds us that poetry offers far more than skill: 'its object is truth' ('Preface' to *Lyrical Ballads*). Poetry can make men wise by speaking to the heart. In *Adonais*, his lament for Keats, Shelley mourns his friend and regrets the loss to poetry. But Keats has escaped sorrow:

> He has outsoared the shadow of our night;
> Envy and calumny and hate and pain,
> And that unrest which men miscall delight,
> Can touch him not and torture not again;
> From the contagion of the world's slow stain
> He is secure, and now can never mourn
> A heart grown cold, a head grown gray in vain.

Life 'stains the white radiance of Eternity', Shelley writes in a later stanza. A Platonic vision of our world as a shadowy reflection of reality is present here, and also the darker Romantic view of this world as a prison for the soul. Shelley's 'calumny' refers to the reviewers who had attacked Keats's work. We might be reminded of Keats's own lines on suffering in 'Ode to a Nightingale'.* The blend of melancholy and consolation in this passage would be impressive on a first reading; but *Adonais* repays study. The verse (this is part of a Spenserian stanza) is skilfully, unobtrusively handled. A knowledge of the tradition of pastoral elegy to which the poem belongs and of Romantic poetry in general helps to narrow the distance between the student and the poem as a whole.

W. B. Yeats said that we use rhetoric when we quarrel with others and make poetry when we quarrel with ourselves. *In Memoriam* (1850), a Victorian elegy in a new form, shows Tennyson quarrelling with himself after the death of an admired and loved friend. Nature, the poem says, is indifferent to individual lives, and perhaps to the whole species. Geological research had recently taught Tennyson's contemporaries that thousands of species, of which fossils preserve traces, have become extinct. Section 56 of *In Memoriam* contemplates the end of Man. Shall Man...

> Who trusted God was love indeed,
>   And love Creation's final law –
>   Though Nature, red in tooth and claw
> With ravine, shrieked against his creed –

---

*See p. 87.

> Who loved, who suffered countless ills,
>   Who battled for the True, the Just,
>   Be blown about the desert dust,
> Or sealed within the iron hills?

The lines express the personal anguish and doubt of the poet, and a dilemma of the period. There is a longing to believe in God, here and throughout *In Memoriam*. Man is heroic in faith despite laws of nature whose hostile presence seems to contradict it. In the time scale of the desert dust and iron hills the extinction of man may not be far off. Other species have been sealed in the hills. The long mournful sentence which spans the quatrain ends with the imagined burial of humanity. The tragic feeling reflects Tennyson's bereavement but it comes from a conflict between doubt and a need to believe. *In Memoriam* reveals the first impact on civilisation of the discovery that man's place in the universe is minute. The poem also teaches how painfully we are sometimes obliged to disagree with ourselves.

Like Milton, T. S. Eliot expected his readers to be students of poetry. He made a technique of quoting from and alluding to other poets in his poems, and in his criticism he redefined tradition – which it is the poet's duty, he said, to renew by working with language:

>   And so each venture
> Is a new beginning, a raid on the inarticulate
> With shabby equipment always deteriorating
> In the general mess of imprecision of feeling,
> Undisciplined squads of emotion.
>
> ('East Coker')

Language may wear out as weapons do; the 'inarticulate' – or what is beyond ordinary description, whether Satan's throne or Keats's immortality – has always been the business of poets; emotions and feelings have always been insubordinate. We study poetry to learn about ourselves and to see language at its best – raiding the inarticulate.

You may have different ideas of your own. You may quote more briefly from major poems, which the examiner will know, and refer to passages which you partly remember. Quote where you can, and always make it clear that your ideas come from knowledge of literature.

Essay topics

Try the following questions which are related to topics covered in the Handbook.

1. Illustrate the use of classical myth in English poetry.
2. How has religious belief influenced the course of English literature?
3. How did Shakespeare learn from other writers?
4. Why are epic poems no longer written?
5. Can we account for the rise of the novel?
6. Why should the novel have been thought disreputable?
7. What do you understand by 'Romanticism'? Illustrate your answer from poems of the Romantic period.
8. How has Romanticism affected later writers?
9. Are special terms necessary for literary criticism?
10. Does metre matter?
11. Discuss the first chapter of a novel or the first scene of a play you know well.
12. Illustrate the treatment of contrasted characters in fiction or drama.
13. Illustrate and comment on misunderstanding in two or more of Shakespeare's comedies (or in any two comedies).
14. Why do we study novels?
15. What is involved in adapting a novel for the stage?
16. What is meant by 'point of view' in fiction?
17. In what sense can a novel be tragic?
18. Do works of literature which have common themes necessarily have anything else in common?

Part 5

Suggestions for reading

Reference books

The following dictionaries are published by Oxford University Press, Oxford:
    In addition to a good dictionary of current English (The *Concise Oxford* or the *Pocket Oxford*), The *Oxford Dictionary of English Etymology*, edited by C. T. Onions, 1966, and H. W. Fowler, *A Dictionary of Modern English Usage*, revised by Sir Ernest Gowers, 1968, are books to own. The *Oxford Companion to English Literature*, compiled and edited by Sir Paul Harvey, revised edition, 1967, is an invaluable dictionary of authors, titles, characters, terminology, myths, and legends.

Ancient literature and mythology

GRAVES, ROBERT: *The Greek Myths*, 2 vols., Penguin Books, Harmondsworth, 1969.
KITTO, H. D. F.: *The Greeks*, Penguin Books, Harmondsworth, 1969.

Translations of Greek and Latin authors are available in Penguin Classics. The New English Library also publishes translations in Mentor Books, New York. E. V. Rieu's translations of Homer's *Iliad* and *Odyssey*, in Penguin, and William Arrowsmith's translation of Aristophanes's *The Birds*, in Mentor Books, are especially good.

Medieval English Literature

Part 1 of the *Oxford Anthology of English Literature*, edited by J. B. Trapp, Oxford University Press, New York, 1973, covers Medieval English Literature.
    The following are readable modern English versions:

Beowulf, translated by Burton Raffel, New English Library, Mentor Books, London and New York, 1963.
Sir Gawain and the Green Knight, translated by Burton Raffel, New English Library, Mentor Books, London and New York, 1970.
CHAUCER, GEOFFREY: *The Canterbury Tales*, translated by Neville Coghill, Penguin Books, Harmondsworth, 1951, revised 1977.

CHAUCER, GEOFFREY: *Troilus and Criseyde*, translated by Neville Coghill, Penguin Books, Harmondsworth, 1971.

The Works of Geoffrey Chaucer, edited by F. W. Robinson, Oxford University Press, Oxford, 1957, is a standard collected edition for those ready to go on to read Chaucer in Middle English. *The Nun's Priest's Tale*, edited by Maurice Hussey, Cambridge University Press, London, 1965, makes a pleasant introduction. John Speirs, *Chaucer the Maker*, Faber & Faber, London, 1951, provides critical assistance.

Medieval poetry can be approached in Douglas Gray, *Themes and Images in the Mediaeval English Religious Lyric*, Routledge, London, 1972. This is a critical study which quotes and comments on the best poems.

For medieval drama, see:

CAWLEY, A. C. (ED.): *Everyman and Medieval Miracle Plays*, Dent, London, 1956.
THOMAS, R. G. (ED.): *Ten Miracle Plays*, Northwestern University Press, Evanston, 1968.

Shakespeare: texts

The Arden editions of Shakespeare published by Methuen, London, are the best for private study. A good one-volume edition of Shakespeare is *The Complete Works*, edited by Peter Alexander, Collins, London, 1951.

Background to Shakespeare

BENTLEY, G. E.: *Shakespeare: A Biographical Handbook*, Yale University Press, New Haven, 1961.
BURGESS, ANTHONY: *Shakespeare*, Penguin Books, Harmondsworth, 1972. A lavishly illustrated account of Shakespeare and his time.
CHAMBERS, E. K.: *William Shakespeare*, 2 vols., Oxford University Press, Oxford, 1930. A very detailed, authoritative study.
SHOENBAUM, S.: *William Shakespeare: A Compact Documentary Life*, Oxford University Press, Oxford, 1977.
WELLS, STANLEY: *Shakespeare: The Writer and his Work*, Longman for the British Council, Harlow, 1978. A brief, illustrated introduction.

Shakespeare criticism

ANDREWS, W. T. (ED.): *Critics on Shakespeare*, 'Readings in Literary Criticism', Allen & Unwin, London, 1973. Includes critical views from the sixteenth century to the present.
BRADLEY, A. C.: *Shakespearean Tragedy*, Macmillan, London, 1905, 1978.

CLEMEN, W. H.: *The Development of Shakespeare's Imagery*, Methuen, London, 1966.
COLERIDGE, S. T.: *Coleridge on Shakespeare*, edited by Terence Hawkes, Penguin Books, Harmondsworth, 1969.
KNIGHT, G. WILSON: *The Wheel of Fire: Interpretations of Shakespearean Tragedy*, Methuen, London, 1949.
MAHOOD, M. M.: *Shakespeare's Word Play*, Methuen, London, 1957, 1968.
MUIR, KENNETH: *The Sources of Shakespeare's Plays*, Methuen, London, 1977.

Modern literature: general

Selections are recommended below (under their various categories), since this is a guide to 'outside' reading. York Notes provide advice on major editions and on background studies for individual texts. Capacious anthologies such as *The Oxford Anthology of English Literature* offer extended reading and good selections in a convenient form. But pocket selections make it easier to concentrate on each writer. Some paperback selections are suggested below, and some titles to begin with. Explore libraries and bookshops for yourself. Borrow background books and, perhaps, novels. Own as much poetry as possible. Favourite poems should be reread often. Novels and plays should be read in bulk. A slim volume of poems can cost little more than a magazine.

Poetry

Paradise Lost includes some of the best poetry in English, but many passages are dull on first encounter. H. S. Taylor's *From Paradise Lost: Selections from John Milton's Poem*, Heinemann Educational Books, London, 1965, is a sensible abridgement with which to start Milton. Nobody reads *Paradise Lost* for the plot. There are many editions of Milton's complete works. *Complete Poems and Major Prose*, edited by Merrit Y. Hughes, Odyssey Press, Indianapolis, is very well annotated indeed. *Selected Poems of Alexander Pope*, edited by John Heath-Stubbs, Heinemann, London, 1964, is a well-chosen selection. Heinemann's 'Poetry Bookshelf' series offers annotated selections from the work of many other major poets. Penguin Books and Faber publish good paperback anthologies. The following collections are especially recommended: *The Metaphysical Poets*, edited by Helen Gardner, Penguin Books, Harmondsworth, 1957; *The Penguin Book of Eighteenth Century Verse*, edited by Dennis Davison, Penguin Books, Harmondsworth, 1973; *The Oxford Book of English Verse of the Romantic Period*, chosen by H. S. Milford, The Clarendon Press, Oxford, 1935, 1974; *The Faber Book of Modern Verse*, edited by Michael Roberts, Faber,

London, 1965; *The New Poetry*, edited by A. A. Alvarez, Penguin Books, Harmondsworth, 1962.

Drama

Penguin, Faber, Macmillan, and Methuen publish relatively inexpensive editions of plays. For those unsure where to start, and perhaps unused to seeing plays acted, the following are recommended (in order of composition): John Webster, *The White Devil*, edited by Elizabeth M. Brennan, Ernest Benn, London, 1966; John Dryden, *All for Love*, edited by N. J. Andrew, Ernest Benn, London, 1975; R. B. Sheridan, *The School for Scandal*, edited by C. J. L. Price, Oxford University Press, London, 1971; Oscar Wilde, *The Importance of Being Earnest*, Eyre Methuen, London, 1966; Sean O'Casey, *Juno and the Paycock*, Samuel French, London, 1968; Samuel Beckett, *Waiting for Godot*, Faber, London, 1956; Harold Pinter, *The Caretaker*, Eyre Methuen, London, 1960.

Fiction

Most of the novels mentioned or discussed in the text are cheaply available in Penguin editions. Among recent novels John Fowles's *The French Lieutenant's Woman* (1969), published in paperback by Panther Triad, London, 1977, is an entertaining work which should interest all students of modern and of Victorian fiction. It looks at the nineteenth century from a modern point of view. After reading William Golding's *Lord of the Flies*, you might try *The Inheritors* (1955) or *The Spire* (1964); Golding's novels are published by Faber & Faber, London.

General criticism

ALLEN, WALTER: *The English Novel*, Penguin Books, Harmondsworth, 1970.
BRADBURY, MALCOLM: *What is a Novel?*, Edward Arnold, London, 1969.
BURGESS, ANTHONY: *Language Made Plain*, revised edition, Fontana Collins, London, 1975.
COX, C. B. and DYSON, A. E.: *The Practical Criticism of Poetry: A Textbook*, Edward Arnold, London, 1965.
FORSTER, E. M.: *Aspects of the Novel*, Penguin Books, Harmondsworth, 1970.
LEAVIS, F. R.: *Revaluation: Tradition and Development in English Poetry*, Penguin Books, Harmondsworth, 1972.
LEECH, CLIFFORD: *Tragedy*, Methuen, London, 1970.
LERNER, LAURENCE: *An Introduction to English Poetry*, Edward Arnold, London, 1975.

REES, R. J.: *English Literature: An Introduction for Foreign Readers*, Macmillan, London, 1973. A pleasant introduction for English-speaking students as well as for those who read English as a foreign language.

SCHOLES, ROBERT: *Elements of Poetry*, Oxford University Press, New York and London, 1969.

TILLYARD, E. M. W.: *The Elizabethan World Picture*, Penguin Books, Harmondsworth, 1972.

WATSON, GEORGE: *The Discipline of English: A Guide to Critical Theory and Practice*, Macmillan, London, 1978. Includes practical advice and sensible discussion of English literature as a subject for study.

Bibliography and guide to further reading

BATESON, F. W.: *A Guide to English Literature*, second edition, Longman, London, 1967.

Index

For myths and for critical terms see the glossaries in Part 2. For Greek, Latin, medieval, and modern names not in the index, consult the appropriate sections of Part 2.

Addison, Joseph, 46, 48, 59
allegory, 41, 43, 50, 54, 121, 123
alliterative verse, 38
Aristotle, 31–2, 40, 46, 70–1
Arthurian romance, 38–9
Austen, Jane, 9, 49, 90, 94, 107–10; *Pride and Prejudice*, 9, 107–10

Bacon, Francis, 9, 47, 125, 127
Beckett, Samuel, 81, 135
Bede, 36
Beowulf, 34, 132
Bible, 7, 34, 36–7, 41, 47
Blake, William, 51
Brooke, Rupert, 61, 106
Boswell, James, 51
Brontë, Charlotte, 9, 90
Brontë, Emily, 53, 90
Browne, Sir Thomas, 45
Browning, Robert, 58, 88
Bunyan, John, 50, 123
Butler, Samuel, *Hudibras*, 61; *Erewhon*, 71
Byron, George Gordon, Viscount, 52–3

Chaucer, Geoffrey, 34, 35, 37, 39–40, 65; *The Canterbury Tales*, 37, 39–40, 60, 132; *Troylus and Cryseyde*, 39, 133
Coleridge, S. T., 8, 51, 52, 53, 55, 63, 88
concordances, 73, 80
Congreve, William, 46, 81
Conrad, Joseph, 60

courtly love, 38–9
critics, 8–9, 32, 72, 73, 80, 91–2, 95–6, 133–4, 135–6

Dante, 40, 70
Defoe, Daniel, 48, 49
Dickens, Charles, 64, 68, 90, 91, 92–3, 94, 95; *Great Expectations*, 91, 92–3, 94, 95; *Oliver Twist*, 90–1
dictionaries, 9, 10, 73, 132
Donne, John, 44, 45, 63
Dryden, John, 46, 47, 49, 50, 51, 52, 135

Eliot, George, 90
Eliot, T. S., 6, 8, 53, 65, 81, 88–9, 125–6, 130, 133
English language, 34–5, 42, 47–9, 84, 98–9, 101–2, 109, 127, 130, 132
epic, 6–7, 30, 34, 36, 43–4, 49, 58–9, 127–8

Fielding, Henry, 48–9, 91, 94
French literature, 38–9, 42, 45–6, 52, 55, 77

Golding, William, 7, 92, 135; *Lord of the Flies*, 119–24
Gray, Thomas, 58
Greek literature, 5–7, 29–32, 39, 43, 57, 59, 61, 66, 132

Herbert, George, 45
Hobbes, Thomas, 50, 121, 123
Homer, 11, 30, 33, 49, 58, 132

138 · Index

Hopkins, Gerard Manley, 60, 69

Italian literature, 40, 41, 42, 43, 77

James, Henry, 91, 92; *Daisy Miller*, 93–4
Johnson, Samuel, 8, 50–1
Jonson, Ben, 44–5, 46, 57, 80

Keats, John, 52, 64, 85–9, 125, 126, 128–9; *'Ode to Autumn'*, 66, 85–7; *'Ode to a Nightingale'*, 87

Lamb, Charles, 59
Latin literature, 5, 32–3, 39, 40, 42, 43, 49–50, 56, 58–9, 64, 132
Lawrence, D. H., 9–10, 53, 91, 94; *Women in Love*, 94
libraries, use of, 5, 9, 10, 33, 72, 73
Locke, John, 48
Lyly, John, 42, 59

Marlowe, Christopher, 42, 80
metaphysical poetry, 40, 44, 45, 134
metre, 8, 49, 60, 63, 68, 86, 88, 89, 105
Middle English literature, 7, 36–40, 42, 51, 52, 132
Miller, Arthur, 81
Milton, John, 6–7, 32, 43–4, 52, 66, 134; *Areopagitica*, 44, 63; *Comus*, 43, 63; *Lycidas*, 43, 58, 61; *Paradise Lost*, 6–7, 43–4, 51, 58, 65, 127–8
Miracle plays, 36–7, 42, 64, 133
mnemonics, 96
mock-epic, 30, 49, 50, 128
More, Sir Thomas, *Utopia*, 41, 71
myth, 5–7, 11–30, 35, 38–9, 44, 53, 64, 128, 131, 132

note-taking, 8–9, 72–6, 82–5, 95–6, 112–15, 120–2, 124–6

Old English literature, 7, 34–5, 132
O'Neill, Eugene, 81
Owen, Wilfred, 105–6

philosophy, 31–2, 37, 42, 45, 47–50, 52, 123

planning written work, *see* note-taking
Plato, 31–2, 45, 52, 125
Pope, Alexander, 33, 47, 49–50, 52, 53, 58, 59, 125, 126, 128, 134
Protestantism, 37, 41–5, 46

Richardson, Samuel, 48–9
Romanticism, 7, 45, 51–4, 85–9, 96, 128–9, 131

satire, 31, 37, 46, 47, 48, 49, 50, 52–3, 94
science, 30, 40, 45, 46–7, 129
Shakespeare, 8, 35, 42–3, 46, 54, 65, 73, 74–80, 111, 112–19, 131, 133–4; life, 74; sources, 76; stage conditions, 77; *Antony and Cleopatra*, 97–102, 120; *Hamlet*, 79, 111, 112–19; *Julius Caesar*, 74, 80, 120; *King Lear*, 6, 74–6, 78–80, 96, 112–19; *Macbeth*, 58, 63, 75, 79, 112–19; *Othello*, 67, 79, 112–19, 127–8; *Twelfth Night*, 77, 79, 113, 118, 119
Shaw, George Bernard, 81, 82, 84
Shelley, Percy Bysshe, 52, 53, 81, 124–5, 126–7, 129; *'Ode to the West Wind'*, 87–9; *'Adonais'*, 129
Sheridan, Richard Brinsley, 46, 63, 81, 83, 135
Sir Gawain and the Green Knight, 38, 132
Smart, Christopher, 50, 51
Soyinka, Wole, 81
Spenser, Edmund, 41–2, 53, 54, 65, 69, 121, 129
Steele, Richard, 46, 48
Sterne, Laurence, 49, 50–1
structuralism, 68, 69
Swift, Jonathan, *Gulliver's Travels*, 47–8, 121, 123
Synge, J. M. 81

Tennyson, Alfred, Lord, 33, 88; *In Memoriam*, 129–30
Thomson, James, 50, 51

unities, 42–3, 45–6, 51–2, 71

Utopia, see *More*

Virgil, 12, 32–3, 37, 40, 43, 49, 50, 58, 128, 132
Voltaire, 52

Webster, John, 80, 135
Wilde, Oscar, 54, 65, 82; *The Importance of Being Earnest*, 81, 83, 102–5, 135
wit, 49, 52–3, 71, 125, 126, 127
Wordsworth, William, 6, 52, 53, 66, 88
Wycherley, William, 46

Yeats, W. B., 6, 7, 53, 125, 129, 134
Young, Edward, 51

The author of this Handbook

NEIL MCEWAN was educated at Pembroke College, Oxford. He has taught English at universities in England, Canada, Cameroon and Morocco. He is now Lecturer in English at the University of Qatar. He has written York Notes on Henry James's *Daisy Miller* and *The Europeans*; D. H. Lawrence's *Women in Love*; Evelyn Waugh's *Decline and Fall*; and L. P. Hartley's *The Go-Between*. He is also the author of *The Survival of the Novel: British Fiction in the Later Twentieth Century*, Macmillan, 1981, and of *Africa and the Novel*, Macmillan, 1983.

York Notes: list of titles

CHINUA ACHEBE
Things Fall Apart
EDWARD ALBEE
Who's Afraid of Virginia Woolf?
ANONYMOUS
Beowulf
Everyman
W. H. AUDEN
Selected Poems
JANE AUSTEN
Emma
Mansfield Park
Northanger Abbey
Persuasion
Pride and Prejudice
Sense and Sensibility
SAMUEL BECKETT
Waiting for Godot
ARNOLD BENNETT
The Card
JOHN BETJEMAN
Selected Poems
WILLIAM BLAKE
Songs of Innocence, Songs of Experience
ROBERT BOLT
A Man For All Seasons
HAROLD BRIGHOUSE
Hobson's Choice
ANNE BRONTË
The Tenant of Wildfell Hall
CHARLOTTE BRONTË
Jane Eyre
EMILY BRONTË
Wuthering Heights
ROBERT BROWNING
Men and Women
JOHN BUCHAN
The Thirty-Nine Steps
JOHN BUNYAN
The Pilgrim's Progress
BYRON
Selected Poems
GEOFFREY CHAUCER
Prologue to the Canterbury Tales
The Clerk's Tale
The Franklin's Tale
The Knight's Tale
The Merchant's Tale
The Miller's Tale
The Nun's Priest's Tale
The Pardoner's Tale
The Wife of Bath's Tale
Troilus and Criseyde
SAMUEL TAYLOR COLERIDGE
Selected Poems
SIR ARTHUR CONAN DOYLE
The Hound of the Baskervilles
WILLIAM CONGREVE
The Way of the World
JOSEPH CONRAD
Heart of Darkness
STEPHEN CRANE
The Red Badge of Courage
BRUCE DAWE
Selected Poems
DANIEL DEFOE
Moll Flanders
Robinson Crusoe
WALTER DE LA MARE
Selected Poems
SHELAGH DELANEY
A Taste of Honey
CHARLES DICKENS
A Tale of Two Cities
Bleak House
David Copperfield
Great Expectations
Hard Times
Oliver Twist
The Pickwick Papers
EMILY DICKINSON
Selected Poems
JOHN DONNE
Selected Poems
GERALD DURRELL
My Family and Other Animals
GEORGE ELIOT
Middlemarch
Silas Marner
The Mill on the Floss
T. S. ELIOT
Four Quartets
Murder in the Cathedral
Selected Poems
The Cocktail Party
The Waste Land
J. G. FARRELL
The Siege of Krishnapur
WILLIAM FAULKNER
The Sound and the Fury

HENRY FIELDING
Joseph Andrews
Tom Jones
F. SCOTT FITZGERALD
Tender is the Night
The Great Gatsby
GUSTAVE FLAUBERT
Madame Bovary
E. M. FORSTER
A Passage to India
Howards End
JOHN FOWLES
The French Lieutenant's Woman
JOHN GALSWORTHY
Strife
MRS GASKELL
North and South
WILLIAM GOLDING
Lord of the Flies
The Spire
OLIVER GOLDSMITH
She Stoops to Conquer
The Vicar of Wakefield
ROBERT GRAVES
Goodbye to All That
GRAHAM GREENE
Brighton Rock
The Heart of the Matter
The Power and the Glory
WILLIS HALL
The Long and the Short and the Tall
THOMAS HARDY
Far from the Madding Crowd
Jude the Obscure
Selected Poems
Tess of the D'Urbervilles
The Mayor of Casterbridge
The Return of the Native
The Woodlanders
L. P. HARTLEY
The Go-Between
NATHANIEL HAWTHORNE
The Scarlet Letter
SEAMUS HEANEY
Selected Poems
ERNEST HEMINGWAY
A Farewell to Arms
The Old Man and the Sea
SUSAN HILL
I'm the King of the Castle
BARRY HINES
Kes
HOMER
The Iliad
The Odyssey

GERARD MANLEY HOPKINS
Selected Poems
TED HUGHES
Selected Poems
ALDOUS HUXLEY
Brave New World
HENRIK IBSEN
A Doll's House
HENRY JAMES
The Portrait of a Lady
Washington Square
BEN JONSON
The Alchemist
Volpone
JAMES JOYCE
A Portrait of the Artist as a Young Man
Dubliners
JOHN KEATS
Selected Poems
PHILIP LARKIN
Selected Poems
D. H. LAWRENCE
Selected Short Stories
Sons and Lovers
The Rainbow
Women in Love
HARPER LEE
To Kill a Mocking-Bird
LAURIE LEE
Cider with Rosie
CHRISTOPHER MARLOWE
Doctor Faustus
HERMAN MELVILLE
Moby Dick
THOMAS MIDDLETON and
   WILLIAM ROWLEY
The Changeling
ARTHUR MILLER
A View from the Bridge
Death of a Salesman
The Crucible
JOHN MILTON
Paradise Lost I & II
Paradise Lost IV & IX
Selected Poems
V. S. NAIPAUL
A House for Mr Biswas
ROBERT O'BRIEN
Z for Zachariah
SEAN O'CASEY
Juno and the Paycock
GEORGE ORWELL
Animal Farm
Nineteen Eighty-four

York Notes: list of titles

JOHN OSBORNE
Look Back in Anger
WILFRED OWEN
Selected Poems
ALAN PATON
Cry, The Beloved Country
THOMAS LOVE PEACOCK
Nightmare Abbey and *Crotchet Castle*
HAROLD PINTER
The Caretaker
SYLVIA PLATH
Selected Works
PLATO
The Republic
ALEXANDER POPE
Selected Poems
J. B. PRIESTLEY
An Inspector Calls
WILLIAM SHAKESPEARE
A Midsummer Night's Dream
Antony and Cleopatra
As You Like It
Coriolanus
Hamlet
Henry IV Part I
Henry IV Part II
Henry V
Julius Caesar
King Lear
Macbeth
Measure for Measure
Much Ado About Nothing
Othello
Richard II
Richard III
Romeo and Juliet
Sonnets
The Merchant of Venice
The Taming of the Shrew
The Tempest
The Winter's Tale
Troilus and Cressida
Twelfth Night
GEORGE BERNARD SHAW
Arms and the Man
Candida
Pygmalion
Saint Joan
The Devil's Disciple
MARY SHELLEY
Frankenstein
PERCY BYSSHE SHELLEY
Selected Poems
RICHARD BRINSLEY SHERIDAN
The Rivals

R. C. SHERRIFF
Journey's End
JOHN STEINBECK
Of Mice and Men
The Grapes of Wrath
The Pearl
LAURENCE STERNE
A Sentimental Journey
Tristram Shandy
TOM STOPPARD
Professional Foul
Rosencrantz and Guildenstern are Dead
JONATHAN SWIFT
Gulliver's Travels
JOHN MILLINGTON SYNGE
The Playboy of the Western World
TENNYSON
Selected Poems
W. M. THACKERAY
Vanity Fair
J. R. R. TOLKIEN
The Hobbit
MARK TWAIN
Huckleberry Finn
Tom Sawyer
VIRGIL
The Aeneid
ALICE WALKER
The Color Purple
KEITH WATERHOUSE
Billy Liar
EVELYN WAUGH
Decline and Fall
JOHN WEBSTER
The Duchess of Malfi
OSCAR WILDE
The Importance of Being Earnest
THORNTON WILDER
Our Town
TENNESSEE WILLIAMS
The Glass Menagerie
VIRGINIA WOOLF
Mrs Dalloway
To the Lighthouse
WILLIAM WORDSWORTH
Selected Poems
WILLIAM WYCHERLEY
The Country Wife
W. B. YEATS
Selected Poems